Sonovagun Stew

PUBLICATIONS OF
THE TEXAS FOLKLORE SOCIETY
NUMBER XLVI

Sonovagun Stew

A FOLKLORE MISCELLANY
edited by Francis Edward Abernethy

SOUTHERN METHODIST UNIVERSITY PRESS

LIBRARY OF CONGRESS CATALOGUING-IN-PUBLICATION DATA
Main entry under title:

Sonovagun stew.

    (Publications of the Texas Folklore Society; no. 46)
    Includes index.
    1. Folklore—Texas—Addresses, essays, lectures.
2. Texas—Social life and customs—Addresses, essays,
lectures. I. Abernethy, Francis Edward. II. Series.
GR1.T4 no. 46   390 s [398.2' 09764]   85-14290
[GR110.T5]
ISBN 0-87074-211-6

Contents

Preface

by Francis Edward Abernethy

In which the editor justifies the title of this publication with a learned discussion of sonovaguns, jambalayas, mulligans, and slumgullions—among other things.

Once upon a time up in Panola County we made one sonovabitch of a stew—which I shall politely refer to hereafter as a sonovagun stew. Some kinfolks of Alfred Jernigan's were having an all-day squirrel hunt and sonovagun stew on their place on the Sabine River. The family had an old shed roof of a camp on the river bank where they gathered to fish, hunt, play dominoes, or drink, according to the season. They had an assortment of tables and chairs and cooking equipment, an iron skillet and a blue enamel coffee pot and a syrup bucket of forks and spoons. A container of grease, another of corn meal, and salt-and-pepper shakers in an orange-crate shelf showed that they were prepared to cook a squirrel or catfish on an instant. And in the middle of the campground—on this cool clean October day before the world got so crowded—squatted a smoked-black, cast-iron wash pot, one foot gone, just waiting to boil a missionary, make lye soap, or host a very large stew.

Three of us splash-banged down an old logging road in Alfred's '39 Chevy, dodging stumps and praying through mudholes and finally got to the camp. A half-a-dozen men—as compared to us early-twenties boys—were sitting around a fire. Two were cleaning squirrels; two others were telling them how; two were refereeing the operation. Alfred, who was younger than Hubert and I but acted older, introduced us around and gave us a couple of beers out of an iced washtub to show that he was one of the official hosts. We stood around awhile until we got Alfred settled down by the campfire; then we got off to the woods.

We had a good hunt. There was a lot of mast that year, and the leaves had fallen enough that you could see to get a shot. We hunted along the road—Hubert on one side, I on the other—so we wouldn't wander off in the wrong direction and then whistled each other in about dark. It was good dark by the time we got back, and the camp was settled down in another dimension, ringed by trees, in firelight and long shadows, with voices bouncing out into the darkness. They had set the wash pot on the fire and had it cradled in rocks so it wouldn't tip over. An old pickup and a jeep had arrived with more Jernigans, and everybody was laughing and talking and doing things to the pot.

We skinned our squirrels and quartered them and tossed them in the pot. The stock was already boiling and squirrel parts were cooking tender. Somebody had tossed in some young cat squirrels, heads and tails, and they periodically rolled to the surface to see what was coming next. A young coon and a rabbit were added to the pot, and some uncle threatened the stew with an armadillo that was snuffling around in the brush just outside the firelight.

When the meat started coming off the bones, the cooks—everybody there— added carrots, potatoes, onions, and God knows what else, canned or cut. One old man kept seasoning the broth with cigar ashes. Other creative souls contributed splashes of beer, whiskey, and coffee "to add character," they said, to the mixture. I heard somebody say, "Dammit, Casey, quit spittin' in that pot." I'm sure he was just joking with those of us who were new to the tradition.

I was starving to the point of eating my hat and gloves when the head cook forked into a piece of meat and finally announced that the stew was ready. We all lined up with a variety of bowls, cups, and coffee cans while the cook ladled it out. It didn't look like the stew you have around the house, probably because there was so much of it, but it smelled about the same, maybe a little stronger. Hubert and I looked over at each other when we sat down to eat, wondering how much of a new experience our stomachs would stand. Alfred was already slurping away as if he had washpot sonovagun at every meal. We might have hesitated but the moment was short, and we ate with hunger whetted appetites. My God, but that was a good stew! I don't know how to describe how good that stew was except to say that that stew took place about forty years ago and I can still savor it on tongue and palate. Everybody was eating and carrying on about how good it was, and the whole scene was like a communion, with people sitting on the edge of the firelight, with stars sparkling on the blue-black sky and owls six-feet tall hoo-haing across the river at each other.

We ate all of it before we got through. In the final stages we were dipping soup and straining the pot for any animal parts that might have escaped the earlier ladlings—and wishing like hell that we had put in the armadillo.

That sonovagun does not square with recipes and descriptions I've encountered of West Texas chuckwagon sonovagun stew—which uses every part of a fat calf except his hide, horns, and hooves—but it is built on the same principle. And this use of whatever is edible and handy is the common denominator of a long standing, traditional run of stews.

The French folks over in Louisiana have their version of a sonovagun, which they call a jambalaya and which I once encountered under interesting circumstances.

Right after I got out of the Navy in '46 I worked a short haul on the *Forty Fathom*, a shrimp boat out of Morgan City, Louisiana. I washed dishes, hosed and swabbed the deck, and headed shrimp for what little pay I got—enough, by the way, to buy my first guitar, a second-hand Stella. The cook was one of Justin Wilson's "smart Cajuns from New Roads," who had recently gotten control of the word *perceive* and used it every time he should have said *see*. In spite of which, he could cook fish more ways and better than any I have tasted since. We had trout, pompano, and snapper and once dragged the try net over an oyster reef and nearly foundered eating raw oysters dipped in some kind of pink sauce he concocted.

We were lying off the mouth of the Atchafalaya one evening when the cook decided he wanted to fry up some venison backstrap. He got his headlight and an old beat-up .30-30, and in the black dark we rowed a pirogue over the flat swells and then through the nastiest mess of water hyacinths that a family of cotton-mouth moccasins ever bedded down in. The cook "perceived" a pair of deer eyes shining back at him in the dark and stepped out of the pirogue on what he thought was true ground. He immediately sank through floating slush to his armpits. We went back to the *Forty Fathom*, hosed him off, and had beer and boiled shrimp.

We always had boiled shrimp on hand. The cook boiled it in an old bucket, and the sweet time of the day was when we sat on the fantail in the evening drinking a beer and grazing on boiled shrimp. Now I remember that! And I remember his jambalaya, which was just a Cajun sonovagun. His jambalaya was darker than Texas sonovagun and thicker because he added rice sometime during the cooking process. He was very casual about his cooking and put into the jambalaya whatever meats were handy—ham, spam, whatever—but shrimp and chicken (there seemed to be a lot of wings) dominated the completed dish. He served it in big bowls with hard-crusted bread, and we sat on the bitts and ate like we were having dinner at Antoine's.

The following summer I sailed out of Ketchikan on the *Pride of Juneau*, a salmon boat, as cook and seine hauler, and I became acquainted with a salmon mulligan, an Alaskan sonovagun. I wasn't much of a cook, but the three-man crew would have put up with Filthy McNasty himself not to have to cook, wash dishes, and keep the galley clean. The *Pride* was thirty-six feet long, and the galley was in the forward part of the cabin, which also held our sleeping quarters. The stove was a simple device, and heat was maintained by firing diesel oil that dripped on a pair of porous bricks. Once in the Gulf of Alaska in the iceberg water below the Bering Glacier, I wide-opened the diesel petcock to get the stove heated in a hurry, then forgot all about it during the flouring of breaded veal cutlets and some lurid fantasizing about my sweetheart back in Texas. I came back to the real world which included a cherry-red-hot stove and paint smoking and bubbling on the bulkhead. Rocky was dousing water on the outside, and the skipper (whom we appropriately called "Bligh") was cursing and flinging flour in on the fire and trying to shut off the still dripping valve. I remained in a conscious but suspended state and continued to automatically flour the veal cutlets during the commotion. After things settled down I was bothered more by my reaction to the incident than I was by the mistake I made—or the fine cussing I got from the skipper.

As a cook I couldn't have gotten anything but better, and the crew was satisfied with the chow, instructing me regularly on what to cook and how to do it. One memorable dish was fresh sardines, fried crisp and eaten whole— lips, livers, and lights. I did various things to fresh salmon and regularly fixed what the crew called a salmon mulligan. It was another version of a sonovagun. I boiled the salmon with potatoes and at the critical time put in whatever canned goods we had in the food locker—corn, peas, carrots, tomatoes. I remember those mulligans fondly and wonder sometimes if a salmon mulligan would taste as good now as it did during those salad days on the Gulf of Alaska.

In my early wanderings I encountered another type of sonovagun, called a slumgullion, but knew it only by reputation. I was on the road and stopped one night to enjoy the hospitality of the Salvation Army in Jacksonville, Florida. The sleeping quarters was a large barn-like room over the mission, with double-deck bunks, barracks style, and I sociably bedded down near two old drifters. I think as much for my benefit as for memory's sake they talked long into the night about their adventures on the road, hopping freights, outsmarting the bulls, just getting by during the hard-times Thirties.

Most of their energies during those Depression years were spent getting food, and times happened when they welcomed a vagrancy charge just to get something to eat and a warm night's sleep. During the good times when the weather was tolerable and the skies were dry, they and their fellow knights would camp at a hobo jungle on the edge of a town, usually near a railroad track, and have a slumgullion. In preparation for the event all would sally forth in search of ingredients. They wandered alleys, both residential and commercial, looking through garbage cans for vegetables in any state of use. They raided gardens, and they stole where possible, at night gently lifting a chicken off its roost and tucking its head under its wing to prevent an outcry. If they were successful panhandling on the steets, they bought a little stew meat. Some preferred door-to-door bumming, knowing that many a Christian housewife wouldn't deny them a handout for fear of "turning away an angel, unaware." At day's end the collection of foods was pooled and a great slumgullion was cooked to the delight and gustatory satisfaction of all the denizens of the jungle. The two old souls reminisced happily about the good old days, before the demands of World War II had forced them into an assortment of jobs and a rash of insensitive bosses. I listened respectfully, agreed that it was bad to have to work for the likes of those who were always put in charge, and honestly wished I could have sat in with them when they had made a real slumgullion.

All this reminiscing sounds as if I'm setting myself up as the galloping gourmet of the stewpot, but that's not the case. I got to be a pretty good cook on the *Pride,* and I sharpened my skills during another year of bachelorhood, but I gave up cooking when I got married. I sure didn't intend to spoil what promised to be a real good wife by horning in on her kitchen duties.

And I hope that readers will understand the significance of the title of this forty-sixth volume of the Society's publication. This is one of our traditional literary sonovaguns and the cook has put into it whatever was savory and on hand—everything but the horns, the hide, and the hooves. I hope that you enjoy partaking of it as much as I did the building of it.

For the tenth time since I became editor in 1971 I thank the Society members whose literary involvements in folklore have resulted in interesting, readable, publishable articles. You keep the Society alive.

The Texas Folklore Society thanks William R. Johnson, President of Stephen F. Austin State University, and Roy E. Cain, Chairman of the Department of English and Philosophy, for continuing financial and moral support. And I thank Marlene Adams, the Society's secretary, for holding off from having her baby until she got these manuscripts to the publisher.

Stephen F. Austin State University
Nacogdoches, Texas

The editor as stew-cook on the *Pride of Juneau,* in the Gulf of Alaska, 1947

Sonovagun Stew

John Graves of Glen Rose, The Dean of Texas Writers (*Reproduced by permission of David Stark © 1984*)

Folklore and Me

by John Graves

Delivered before the Texas Folklore Society at Huntsville, April 1, 1984.

The title of this speech isn't a very sparkling one, chiefly because I arrived here with an untitled sheaf of paper and Professor Stewart asked me what I was going to call it. In connection with this, I guess I'd better reassure both the laymen and the folklore experts among you by saying that I have no intention of trying to talk learnedly about folklore to an audience as heavily laced with real folklorists as this one. Any writer is a presumptuous person by necessity, in that he presumes he's got something to say and that other people are going to want to hear it. But there are limits to presumption. I'm not a dedicated folklorist; I'm a writer. Sometimes these two things can be combined in a single fellow, as they were for instance in one of the patron saints of the Texas Folklore Society, J. Frank Dobie, and as they are in Bill Owens, who spoke to you this afternoon. But I think that quite often they aren't combinable in that way; in fact, they can conflict with each other in ways that I will be examining at some point in this talk.

What folklore has mainly meant to me, and what I think it most usually means to writers who have any connection with it, is *material* to be used in pieces of writing that in one way or another make the writer's own personal points. That is, it's a subordinate element, not a point in itself, and since folklore generally has its own point to make, that point sometimes has to be subjugated to the author's intention. We writers are thus often perverters, in a sense, of folklorists' sacred texts.

The kind of folk material that has interested me most—the kind, that is, that I've found most useful—is really factual stuff, the recount of events and friendships and hostilities and so forth that may have had little impact

3

beyond the limits of a family, or a neighborhood, or a county, or a small region. In a way it's history, but an intimate kind of history passed down most often by word of mouth over the years and transmuted in the telling by each generation, sometimes by each individual teller. So in the end it is no longer pure history but legend, in that it may reflect not what really happened but what a family or a people *want* to have happened, and therefore in a sense what that family or that people are, or what they aspire to be. I would guess that you folklorists are far more familiar than I am with this process, since it is one thing that produces all the variant versions and corruptions of anecdotes and stories in which you often interest yourselves.

The friends of this kind of lore, it seems to me, are those who love storytelling and accuracy, wherever it happens to lead. One main set of its enemies—besides us corruptive writers—consists of those who always want to make things look nice, for genteel or genealogical reasons, emphasizing what is respectable, or heroic, or at worst picturesque, and deleting everything scandalous, or shady, or bawdy, or lower-class—the kind of stuff that's likely to be of special interest to pokers and pryers like me. Our own lore in this part of the world often traces back to Victorian times, and much of Victorianism has lingered here into later times, and this means that respectability has often been a prime villain.

The period of Reconstruction in Texas, for instance, with all its feuds and bitterness and vengeful bloodshed, has always been of special interest to me for various reasons, but it is the hardest of all our regional periods to study in terms of facts, because so many of the facts that were recorded were later burned or otherwise destroyed, and those that weren't recorded often perished with the forthright old-timers who might have passed them down but didn't, because their respectable descendants disapproved. In case any of you are wondering, I do know that I'm still mixing up history and folklore here, but in truth the kind of history that I like best and the kind of folklore that I like best can't always be separated.

In the area of North Central Texas where I've lived for a good many years and about which I have often written, there was a remarkable old ex-Ranger named Buck Barry, who came to Bosque County when its population consisted mainly of Indians and who lived there to a ripe old age and wrote down some recollections of all he'd seen and done over the years. They make fine reading, but in them there is hardly anything about Reconstruction, because after he died somebody just took those parts out and did away with them.

In my own father's family lore there was a similar respectable excision concerning one whole branch of the kinship, who were evidently mixed up in the nasty Sutton-Taylor feud down in DeWitt County, a long-continuing brawl that was itself a product of Reconstruction. The one family member who knew about all that and survived into my own time, a spinster schoolteacher known as Cousin Nora Fudge, wouldn't say a word about it. She was a delightful, bright old lady who lived in a little gingerbread house and knew a lot about literature and other good things, and I loved her dearly, but although I badgered her more than once to turn loose of what she knew, it all went with her as a secret to her grave, for respectability's sake.

I know I'm wandering a bit, but folklorists ought to be used to that. Sometimes the old earthy or ungenteel stories do come down, usually through the male line. One that my father used to tell fairly often—mainly, I think, because it never failed to infuriate my mother—was tied in with that same branch of the family upon whose vital data our Cousin Nora Fudge so tightly sat. It's not any very great story but it's ours, which I guess is the main thing that can be said about most family anecdotes. It seems that one of Papa's maternal aunts, long before he was born, had married a thoroughly disreputable, shotgun-assassin, mean-poor-white type known as "Mule" McGill (that nickname is the actual one he bore, but the surname isn't). Anyhow, her family and its connections were so disgruntled by the match that they stopped even talking about her, and my father as a child never heard her name and knew nothing of her existence.

One day when he was about twelve, a circus came to Cuero, and he and his best friend, a boy named Wofford Rathbone, rode their ponies over to watch the big tents being put up. While they were sitting there horseback viewing the spectacle, a very dirty and dishevelled man with a beard came slouching along and stopped to regard them. From Papa's description of him he must have looked a good bit like Huckleberry Finn's horrible sire. He was clearly about half-drunk and was leaking tobacco juice at the corners of his mouth.

He said, "Hello there, Wofford."

"How're you, Mr. McGill," said my father's friend.

"Who's that you got there with you?"

"That's Johnny Graves."

"Johnny Graves!" the apparition said, peering up at Papa. "Why, boy, I'm yore damn *uncle!*"

Papa took a good look at him and hollered, "No, you ain't!" Then he turned his pony and ran it all the way home, where my grandfather told him at long last the story of Uncle Mule.

I've never used that particular family anecdote in any published writing, though I still may do it sometime. I've used other family stuff, and I've used other people's family stories too, when they fitted in with the aim of a piece of writing. I've used a lot of written-down folklore, too. These "borrowings," as the polite phrase goes, are not really borrowings at all, because I'm not going to put them back where I found them. They're thefts. And the flat fact is that writers, in addition to being often perverters of good folk material, are natural-born thieves as well, garnering their subject matter wherever they find it. I'm not talking about plagiarism, which involves expression, but about the world's store of information, which writers think belongs to them. By writing about some item in that store, they do more or less make it their own, and very often, after this process has taken place, they forget entirely where they found it.

One of my short stories that has received a little favorable attention, for instance, is called "The Last Running." It is based on an anecdote I once heard or read somewhere about Charles Goodnight in his old age, when a small band of Comanche Indians rode out from Oklahoma to his Quitaque Ranch below the Cap Rock to ask for one of the buffalo from the little herd he maintained, so that they could run it and kill it in the ancient, traditional way with arrows and lances. It ties up a lot of historical meaning and feeling, this anecdote, and I have used it twice, once in a book in more or less factual, bare-bones form, and later in that short story where I could play with it and shape its meanings. And by the time I got through with it, I had made it so much my own that I didn't, and don't now, have the least idea of where I'd first run across it. By then it was purely mine. I had robbed somebody of it utterly.

Another example of this appropriative process has to do with a tale a friend of mine once told me. He had grown up on a dry-land cotton farm up near Childress or Quanah, and his boyhood existence had not been exactly idyllic. It had in fact been hard, and rough, and poor, and often fraught with uncertainty about such things as food and shoes. One particularly bad autumn, his father took what little cotton they'd made to town, and with the proceeds from it and what other money he could borrow, he loaded up a wagon with a minimum of winter provisions, including a small barrel of molasses, which was absolutely the only sweetening the family would have until spring. When he arrived back at the farm and opened the wagon's tailgate to unload it, the molasses barrel rolled out and busted wide open on the ground. While six children watched in shock, some pigs came running over and lapped up its spilled contents with loud and happy slurping noises. My friend said he would never forget how it drooled down from their chins.

It was a nice sort of story, and I tucked it away in my head, intending to use it whenever I found a place for it. In other words, I was going to steal it for myself. But one time I made the mistake of telling it to Larry McMurtry in the days when I first knew him, at TCU in the early 1960s, and—you guessed it. It turned up in a book of his that came out a couple of years or so later. I didn't mind—we're friends, and I'm a writer and know what writers are like. But at some point when I saw McMurtry and mentioned it to him and teased him a little about the abstraction, he was genuinely indignant. That incident, he insisted, had occurred in his own family. By then he actually believed it had, too.

In still another instance, I myself came out as a sort of villain. When I was digging around for tales and lore in connection with the Brazos River canoe trip that later was the framework for my first book, *Goodbye to a River*, one of the most helpful people I found was a worthy Parker County gentleman named Fred Cotten, whom some of you must have known, since he was later president of the state historical society. He knew pretty much everything there was to know about the history of his immediate region (Parker County was just about it, but he knew it mile by mile), and he was very generous to me with his knowledge, little of which he ever wrote down for publication. I ended up using quite a bit of his lore when I wrote my river book, and I was careful to give him special credit for it and to make certain he received one of the first copies of the book, hot off the presses.

I heard nothing from him about it, however, and a few weeks later I drove out to Weatherford and dropped by his furniture store. He greeted me with noticeable coolness and did not mention the book. Finally I asked if he had received it. He said yes, he had, and he didn't say anything else.

At that point there wasn't any way of getting around asking what he'd thought of it, so I did.

"Well, to tell you the truth, I didn't like it much," he said.

"Why not?"

"Well," said Mr. Cotten, "it just had too much cussing in it."

Any of you who have read that book know that it contains very little strong language or material, possibly less than it ought to contain for authenticity.

I was puzzled, but I didn't argue with him. Some time afterward when I ran into Joe Frantz, then head of the University of Texas history department and an old Weatherford boy who knew Fred Cotten well, I told him what had happened. Joe laughed and laughed and said yes, he'd talked with the old gentleman too. It didn't have much to do with rough language, he said, though Mr. Cotten was a little disturbed by my interest in the off-color aspects of things. What it really amounted to was that he had been sitting for all that time on all that fine material, thinking that someday he might write it down and publish it, but knowing inside that he wouldn't. And even though the other fellow who did write down a little of it and publish it—me—had his full permission, seeing it in that fellow's book had made him mad as hell.

I might note that his "mad" didn't last very long and that before he died we were friendly again. I think that eventually he even took a little pride in his part of the book, though he never, never admitted in my hearing that it was any good. And if all this has a moral, I guess it is that you'd better not tell a writer anything that's important to you. He'll steal it from you if he can. He just can't help himself.

Mainly, of course, when a writer steals such material he's taking it from people who have no notion of ever using it themselves in writing and who most likely will never see it in printed form. These days you can't count on this, however. Even simple people are mainly literate now, and a good number of them believe they have knowledge and stories that are worth a lot of money. This comes from reading in newspapers and magazines about the enormous sums that are paid to a handful of blockbuster authors—the Irving Stones and Judith Krantzes and Harold Robbinses of this world—by movie studios and paperback publishers, and it is based on a widespread belief that the intrinsic cash worth of a piece of writing resides not in its wording and form, as we deluded authors are prone to believe, but in the raw material it contains. I don't suppose there's an established writer in this region, or any other region, who isn't approached one or two or three times a year, or even more often, by someone who proposes that he write a blockbuster best seller based on that someone's experiences in Vietnam, or in the international drug trade, or in the Waco police department, or somewhere else, with the purpose of splitting the huge proceeds between them. Some of these are rather paranoid types. Not long ago I had one fellow come around who couldn't bring himself to do more than hint at what his wonderful story was about, so apprehensive was he that I would swipe it then and there. I don't know how he expected us to get together on the writing of this epic, whatever it was. Finally he just sat there and glared at me for a while, then he got up and left. Maybe somebody had told him about writers being thieves, but really, few of us are *that* bad.

Then, of course, there is the old bugaboo of giving offense by writing down stories that involve real live people, which in its extreme form can lead to libel suits or bodily contusions. In our reasonably literate and extremely communicative society, an author no longer has the freedom to use real-life material at will—as did, for instance, Ivan Turgenev in his superb *A Sportsman's Sketches* which gives accounts of his wanderings through the nineteenth-century Russian countryside and sets down the people he met just as he saw them, warts and idiosyncrasies and all. Books still don't sell and get around as much as we authors would like them to, or we'd all be rich. But some of them do seem to get around to a degree out of all proportion to the puny profits shown on publishers' accounting sheets, and this may be especially true of writers like me whose material is principally gathered in a given region and the bulk of whose readership lives within that region too.

I'm not much addicted to scandal for its own sake, and much of my writing and my use of folk stories has been retrospective—that is, it's about things that took place some time ago, and often about people now dead. Hence I haven't had any libel suits yet, and I haven't had anybody come after me with a pistol or a green-oak club. But you can earn some enemies even if you just fool around with the past and aren't very scandalous. I live in a small, hilly county that was more or less worn-out agriculturally about ninety or a hundred years ago, so that afterward it had to build a very skimpy and tough economy around such arduous activities as the chopping of cedar fence posts and the manufacture of illegal whiskey. It is thus not one of the great book-reading centers of the world. But a surprising number of its inhabitants appear to have read my books, or at least to have read *in* them—mainly, in all likelihood, just because I live there and some of my writing has been about the neighborhood itself. Most seem either to like the books or to be indifferent to them, both of which attitudes suit me fine, especially the latter one of indifference. I am, for whatever strange reasons, one of those peculiar authors who'd just as soon not have anybody he knows ever read anything that he writes. I agree with Gertrude Stein, that much maligned, wise old lady, who once said, "I write for myself and strangers."

Nevertheless, in a little county with the size and population of mine—that is, before the nuclear plant hit us, but that's another story—there aren't very many strangers, and I am occasionally made aware that not everybody within its boundaries is completely delighted with my books. Maybe some think I've stolen their stuff, but I believe it's usually because they think, rightly or wrongly, that they or someone kin to them have been depicted in a not entirely complimentary light, and for many folks, it seems, if a depiction isn't complimentary it must be *un*complimentary. These mild resentments show up in the form of people who don't greet me very warmly at the post office and things like that. Once, after my *Hard Scrabble* book was published, and I was worrying a little about some such occurrence—yes, it does bother me—my state of mind was not in the least soothed when a very sly and furtive old native got me off in a corner and said, "Man, if I'd a known you was going to write *that* kind of a book, I sure could a told you some stories."

Maybe the worst trouble I ever had in this respect, though, came from my use of material from the relatively remote past. This involved the Truitt-Mitchell feud in my area in the 1870s or so, which I utilized in *Goodbye to a River* to symbolize the displacement of the old, direct, rough frontiersmen, the Mitchells, by the more civilized and subtle-minded newcomers as exemplified in the Truitts. There were disagreements and fights and killings, and the patriarch of the Mitchell clan, named Nelson Mitchell but known as Cooney, was publicly hanged in Granbury for his participation, though there was widespread belief then and later that he wasn't any guiltier than anybody else. Then there was some further bloody and dramatic stuff over the years, culminating when Cooney Mitchell's son Bill tracked the Reverend James Truitt to his new home at Timpson in East Texas and shot him out of an armchair while his family looked on. It was all a nice, big, gory, Texas-sized mess.

Anyhow, I read everything I could find about the feud, and I talked with some old-timers, most of whom at least knew things their parents and uncles and aunts had said. I ended up with a bunch of conflicting information, and when I used it in the book, I shaped it and selected from it to suit my purpose—this being, as I've said, to illustrate a specific social change. Even in the text I was frank about doing this, but I guess it made me seem to stand more or less on the side of the Mitchells as opposed to the Truitts. Well, when the book came out it quickly became apparent that while the Mitchells and all their kith and kin had vanished to the four winds, there were members of the Truitt connection just about everywhere, most of them female and one hundred percent genealogically minded. They were great letter writers, too—to me, to my publishers, and elsewhere—and I think I'd rather have been whacked twenty or thirty times with a green-oak club than to have been kept wincing under their verbal assault, which lasted for a year or so. One of them turned out to be the mother of a girl I'd gone with in high school. Maybe one of them is in this audience tonight. If so, and if you want to jump on me after this speech, please do remember that your kinswomen have already exacted a pretty good revenge. I expect that they've cured me of ever again seeming to take sides in any feud that has been waged since Roman times.

That matter of giving offense is one excellent reason for taking up the writing of fiction, and I'm sure it has something to do with the fact that I myself have tried in most of my non-fiction work to maintain a certain freedom to fictionalize when I want to—to change events and names and otherwise to reshape factual material. It isn't the main reason, though. The main reason is related to form and to impact and to that process I mentioned early in this talk, the process of subordinating the authenticity and exactness of material to the writer's own aims. In this connection I referred to writers as perverters of good folklore, and most of them who use it *are* perverters, or ought to be. I believe this is the sharpest point of divergence between genuine folklorists and people who are primarily writers, and it's also the reason that it's quite hard for an individual to be a really good folklorist and a really good writer at one and the same time. The ones who have achieved this best, I think, have tended to alternate their use of these separate talents, putting on one hat for one piece of work, and the other for the next.

I'm not taking sides in this. I place a very great value on authentic folklore validly rendered, not just as material but for its own sweet sake, even if—so far at least—I've had to admire it from the outside, so to speak, and when I've used it I've usually had to corrupt it to some degree, because the shape and drift and point of my own work, whether an essay, or a story, or a book, have continued to be the things that matter most to me. For this individual writer, folk material not only has made the world I know a far, far richer place in which to move around, but also has provided such a huge, wonderful variety of subject matter that if I keep on looting the hoard for the rest of my life, as I probably will, I still won't have made a dent in it. This is a very nice thing for a thief to know. It's like knowing about a great big jewelry store with a back window always open at night.

Bob Wills (*Reprinted by permission from Charles R. Townsend,* San Antonio Rose: The Life and Music of Bob Wills, *1976*)

From Folk to Popular Song to Folklore

THE STORY OF BOB WILLS' "SAN ANTONIO ROSE"

by Charles R. Townsend

In 1927, Bob Wills left Dendy's Barber College in Amarillo and began practicing his newly acquired profession in Roy, New Mexico. While he lived in that little village, he wrote the music that was the basis for the song that made him famous—"San Antonio Rose."[1] As Wills looked back on it, he saw the whole affair as a little ironical, sprinkled perhaps with a bit of fate and a whole lot of luck. Circumstances and immediate necessity actually compelled him to compose the original music. It seemed the people of Roy preferred Bob Wills the musician to Bob Wills the barber. In fact, his barber trade simply did not provide him and his wife with even a meager living. He had to play his fiddle at dances to survive. This was nothing new for him, for when he was just five years old, he began playing for dances. In those early years, his father, John Wills, played fiddle and young Jim Rob "seconded" or played rhythm on mandolin. Jim Rob graduated to guitar, and when he was ten, he played the fiddle at his first dance. Jim Rob played a new kind of music, a music in which he combined the blues, jazz, and ragtime of the East Texas Negroes with the fiddle music his father and grandfather taught him. It was swinging fiddle music and people in East Texas, where he was born, and West Texas, where he grew up and first played it, loved to dance to the music of Bob Wills. But not the people in and around Roy, New Mexico. Wills did not understand this; nor did he appreciate what a fortuitous moment this was in his life.[2]

At the moment, he knew he had to create a music that the people there would find danceable. That part of New Mexico was very isolated and provincial. The population was almost entirely Mexican and Indian. Wills told me that regardless of what music he played, "breakdown fiddle tune, waltz, or two-step, it made little difference. They danced the same way regardless." They did a most unusual dance, much like that of a prairie chicken. Ethno-musicologists refer to the music for such a dance as "chicken scratch," common among some Southwestern Indians.[3] Eventually, Jim Rob came up with the right music. The whole experience in Roy was important for his musical career. First of all, it forced him to write his first composition, which he later entitled "Spanish Two Step." He later rearranged the notes into an American classic, "San Antonio Rose." Finally, he added a third folk music to his repertory, the Spanish or Mexican music of the Southwest.

In the meantime, Jim Bob Wills was merely trying to make a living. The Mexicans and Indians loved his new composition and would dance to nothing else he played. He had to play the "tune over and over again, three or four hours a night." Bob told me: "I got so tired of it I couldn't stand the sound of it. I made up my mind that I'd never play it again when I left New Mexico." The tune would probably have been lost had it not been for Dr. Joe Garner in Turkey, Texas. Bob moved back to West Texas in 1928 and barbered at F. O. Ham's Shop in Turkey. "Old Doc Garner would come in the shop," Bob said, "and would always want me to play 'Big Taters in the Sandyland' and 'Spanish Two Step.' "[4]

The doctor's love of the tune evidently led Jim Bob to keep it in his repertory. In 1929, he moved to Fort Worth, played on various radio stations, and in 1931, organized the Light Crust Doughboys. Bob Wills, as they began referring to him in Fort Worth, occasionally played "Spanish Two Step" on the Doughboy broadcasts. Requests began to come into WBAP for the tune, and Bob knew "it had caught on."[5] In 1935, at his first recording session for Vocalion (later Columbia), he recorded "Doc Garner's old favorite," and it sold very very well. By that time, Wills had added brass and reeds, drums, and piano, and in addition to fiddle music, he was playing a good deal of blues, jazz, race, and pop music. Considering his ability and reputation as a fiddler, Bob recorded relatively few fiddle selections in his first three sessions. In a recording session in May 1938, Wills did not record a single old-time fiddle tune. Arthur Satherley, Columbia's Artist and Repertoire representative who directed Wills' sessions, informed him that Columbia had several bands recording jazz, many Negroes recording race, and even more singers recording pop songs, but they had only one Bob Wills with his fiddle and his Texas Playboys. For the session coming up in November 1938 in Dallas, Satherly demanded "no less than eight fiddle selections."[6]

Between May and November, Bob got busy rehearsing the fiddle tunes, some of which were generations old and were handed down from fiddler to fiddler before Andrew Jackson went to the White House. Some of the selections he recorded in that 1938 session had been part of the ever-receding American frontier from the East Coast to Wills' beloved West Texas. Breakdowns, waltzes, rags—they ran the gamut. During those three days in Dallas, Bob had a field day recording fiddle music. In fact, he recorded more in that session than he had in all his sessions since 1935 combined. In 1938, he still had thirty-five years of his career before him, and for every one of those years, people would request some of the fiddle music he recorded in that November session.

One selection in particular was worth more to his career than all the rest in the session, probably worth more than everything he had ever recorded. It was "old Doc Garner's favorite," the one Bob wrote in New Mexico as "chicken scratch" music, the tune he once wanted neither to hear nor play again. Bob rearranged the music he had written for "Spanish Two Step" into a new composition. It sounded like most recordings of traditional fiddle music, but with the magical jazz beat and swing that Wills always expertly added. Art Satherley loved it: "Bob, what do you call it?" When Bob told him he had no name for the new piece, Satherley said, "I've always loved San Antonio. Let's call it 'San Antonio Rose.' " Bob said he agreed but thought, "What a strange name for a fiddle tune." "Uncle Art," as Bob and the Playboys called him, was way ahead of Wills in his naming of the fiddle tune. Neither Bob nor Uncle Art realized that this was another of the fortuitous incidents in Bob's life. Both the *tune* and the *name* were hits. Since 1935, Bob Wills' recording has sold very well; in fact, *Downbeat* reported in January 1937 that Wills had outsold every artist on the Vocalion label. But he had never had a recording that sold as well as "San Antonio Rose." The nearest to it had been "Trouble in Mind."[7]

"San Antonio Rose" had potential that neither Wills nor Satherley comprehended. Interestingly, it was not anyone in the West, where the music was born, but Irving Berlin, Incorporated, in New York City, that saw the song's possibilities. Irving Berlin and members of his distinguished publishing firm heard the recording and thought the melody was beautiful. Early in the spring of 1940, the Berlin firm contacted Wills about publishing "San Antonio Rose," and Fred Kramer flew to Tulsa to complete the arrangements. O. W. Mayo, Wills' manager, and Kramer went out to Bob's ranch, where Bob was sick and in bed. Bob had had Wayne Johnson write the music, and after they exchanged greetings and talked awhile, Bob handed Kramer the music. Kramer looked at the music approvingly, then asked, "Where are the lyrics?" Bob explained that the song was an instrumental and therefore had no lyrics. Kramer said Berlin was interested in the song only if there were lyrics. Bob and Kramer signed a contract in which Bob agreed to give Irving Berlin, Incorporated the publishing rights, and Kramer agreed to give Wills three hundred dollars in advance royalties. Not that Bob needed the money. He said he knew if they gave him "an advance, they wouldn't put it on a shelf and do nothing with it." The easterner flew back to New York with "San Antonio Rose" by his side. The rest is a story of success for all concerned, with a sprinkling of the comic opera.[8]

Bob had insisted on the three-hundred-dollar advance in order to force Berlin "to do something with the song." Ironically, Bob was the one who had to do something—add the lyrics. As it turned out it was one of the wisest and most significant things he did in his entire career. Without Irving Berlin, he probably would never have done it. Everett Stover, Sleepy Johnson, Tommy Duncan, and others in the band helped Wills write the lyrics. Tommy Duncan came up with some verses first, but they were rejected almost entirely. According to most of the band members, Everett Stover was more help to Wills than anyone else. All sorts of tales and myths about who wrote the lyrics and even who helped write the music have made the rounds. As in the case of every band of the time, when a bandleader added a new selection, several band members helped work out the arrangement. This was true of "San Antonio Rose"; several Texas Playboys contributed to its success, but it was originally a Bob Wills melody, and only his name went on the sheet music. At the time, no great to-do was made about all this. Neither Bob nor any member of his organization had any idea "Dr. Garner's favorite fiddle tune" with lyrics would make musical history.[9]

Much more important to Bob at the time, he had to get the band and the repertory ready for a recording session with Columbia in April 1940 in Dallas. Between his November 1938 session and the 1940 session, Wills had been busy building a big swing band. When he went into the studio to record on April 15, his band included eighteen members: Bob Wills and Jesse Ashlock, violins; Tommy Duncan, vocals; Leon McAuliffe, steel guitar; Louis Tierney, violin and saxophone; Eldon Shamblin, electric guitar; Johnnie Lee Wills, tenor banjo; Herman Arnspiger, guitar; Son Lansford, bass; Al Stricklin, piano; Everett Stover and Tubby Lewis, trumpets; Wayne Johnson, saxophone and clarinet; Zeb McNally, Tiny Mott, Joe Ferguson, and Don

Bob Wills in 1940 at the time he made his first movie and recorded "New San Antonio Rose" (*Reprinted by permission from Townsend*, San Antonio Rose)

Harlan, saxophone; Smokey Dacus, drums. This was the largest Texas Playboy band Bob Wills ever used in a recording session and, if success is a safe barometer, his best.

The recordings the band made during the two-day session reveal why the Playboys were later known as "America's most versatile band." They ran the gamut of American popular music: frontier fiddle music, "Lone Star Rag" and "Brownskin Gal"; blues and race music, "Corrine Corrina" and "Bob Wills Special"; variety, "A Medley of Spanish Waltzes" and "Take me Back to Tulsa"; big-band swing, "Big Beaver," "Wait 'Til You See," and one other.[10]

It was the "one other" that made the 1940 recording session the most epochal in Bob Wills' career. Like "Big Beaver" and "Wait 'Til You See," it was a straight swing band piece, all horns. In fact, Bob's band by 1940 was what was popularly called an orchestra. Bob's last five recordings in the session were in the big-band style of Benny Goodman, Glenn Miller, Bob Crosby, and other swing orchestras of the time. Bob may have recorded them more as a whim, since he thought that Satherley and Columbia might not release them. But here was an eighteen-piece orchestra on salary, ready to play; why not at least let them have a jam session? Their last recording was the selection Wills had recently written lyrics for and sent to Irving Berlin, "San Antonio Rose." Because it had been less than two years since he recorded the original "San Antonio Rose," and because he was adding lyrics, he called it "New San Antonio Rose." It was new in every respect except the melody; it was the fiddle tune dressed up in the most modern musical styles. " 'San Antonio Rose,' " Leon McAuliffe remarked, "we recorded it with a fiddle lead and a steel guitar lead in the middle. 'New San Antonio Rose' had neither." The recording sounded just like those of all the other contemporary swing bands.[11]

The only thing folkish about the recording was the original melody and Bob's folk holler. If he had not hollered the listeners would have thought they were hearing one of the more traditional swing bands of the time. Wills' hollering and talking to his musicians was not, as many believed, show-business facade. It was a musical expression. "Some of those 'ah haas,' " Smokey Dacus said, "you would swear never came out of a human. It just came out and moaned and molded into the music." Bob began this when he was quite young. At the ranch dances in West Texas, his father, grandfather, and the cowboys, too, would give out with a folk yell if the spirit of the music (or the whiskey) so moved them. His wisecracking and talking to his musicians also came from his youth, from his relationships with black musicians who were continually bantering while they performed. The free and uninhibited spirit of his family, the West Texas cowboys, and Texas Negroes had been part of him since his earliest years; it was not something he adopted later. In the recording of "New San Antonio Rose" Bob cried out, "Ah haa, my San Antonio Rose." Since this was his most famous recording, this expression became familiar throughout the nation.[12]

Bob Wills often said that "New San Antonio Rose" was "the song that took us from hamburgers to steaks." [13] This was not exactly the case, but this recording was perhaps the most important moment in his career. An immediate hit in most commercial areas of American popular music, it won Wills a gold record in 1940. The recording eventually sold just over three million discs.[14] From his first session to World War II, Bob recorded more than two hundred selections, but "New San Antonio Rose" did more for him than all the others combined. Without it most of the others would have gone into oblivion, and it is quite possible that Wills and western swing would have been forgotten also.

Though Bob Wills' recording was making musical history, "San Antonio Rose" was not selling well at all for Irving Berlin. When his publishing house received the music and lyrics, they evidently thought the song would not sell as Wills had written it. They wrote Bob's lawyer, David Randolph Milsten, for permission to "rearrange the song to make it a more commercial number." Bob reluctantly agreed. Berlin published its arrangement as " 'San Antonio Rose' by Bob Wills." The lyrics describe a prairie moon hanging low, while the singer addresses the stars above about his sweetheart of the Alamo. He assures her that he will be riding back to her when his "roundup chores" are finished. The lyrics sounded like they were written by a New Yorker who had been no farther west than New Jersey and who had combined lyrics from a song in a Gene Autry movie with an old Vernon Dalhart recording. If this were not enough, Wayne Johnson admitted to me that he got the music mixed up and sent the "harmony rather than the lead part." Apparently this is the way Berlin published the sheet music that he labeled the "Original San Antonio Rose."

Little wonder that Saul H. Bornstein, Berlin's treasurer and general manager, complained about the lack of success with the Berlin version of the song. "We have shown it to about twenty-five prominent orchestra leaders and radio vocalists," Bornstein wrote to Milsten. "We just could not get to first base." Evidently, Wayne Johnson was afraid to tell Bob he had sent the wrong music, for Milsten wrote Bornstein on July 16, 1940: "Mr. Wills did not contemplate such a radical change in the tune. . . . According to Mr. Wills the original tune has been abandoned and the song has been revised so that now all that is heard when playing the piano score is harmony to the original melody." Milsten further complained: "You have so changed the words and the tune that patrons and fans of Bob Wills will not accept the song. Mr. Wills now almost continually has embarrassing moments when his Orchestra plays the song as published because patrons refuse to dance to the tune and call for the original to be played and the original words to be sung." Even after Bornstein received this letter, he continued to believe that Bob's desire to publish the song as he wrote it was unwise. "I don't know whether it would be better in the original form," he wrote in August 1940, "but I am inclined to believe, having had twenty-five years of experience in the business, that it would be more acceptable in the corrected form." In short, Bornstein believed Bob Wills' "San Antonio Rose" was *incorrect* or *wrong* musically.

David Randolph Milsten argued pointedly, passionately, and persuasively in behalf of the original "San Antonio Rose." Bornstein had used a phrase in reference to Bob's original work that showed that Bornstein understood the secret of the song's appeal. Milsten quoted Bornstein's letter that reflected that understanding. "I realized that it was foreign to the everyday popular song, nevertheless, I thought it has that certain something that would stand out. . . ." "That certain something" was in the original interpretation, and without it "San Antonio Rose," as revised by the Berlin firm, was "just another simple song of which there are hundreds on the market," Milsten explained. "Bob Wills is not schooled in the rudiments of music and some of the tunes his orchestra plays would defy the ingenuity of Sigmund Spaeth and yet he has a following which is beyond comprehension." Wills, he continued, "sprang from the ranches of Texas and has built his popularity by his hillbilly personality and 'that certain something' which is reflected in his recordings." He kept reminding Bornstein of his own words of wisdom. "I believe that your original 'hunch,' if I may use such a term, was correct, namely that the original interpretation with 'that certain' swing is the one which will sell the song." Milsten added, "I trust you will see the inconsistency of recordings being made constantly by Bob Wills of the original interpretation and the published interpretation being sold over the counter in music stores."

Milsten was not finished. A postscript—reflecting the same warmth and feeling that Wills put into his music—revealed how Milsten went beyond the call of duty as a lawyer. "Since completing the body of this letter the thought has occurred to me that this entire situation might be likened to the late, beloved Will Rogers. If someone had taken Will and endeavored to school him in the art of public speaking, causing him to lose those treasured eccentricities of speech and mannerisms which he possessed, he would have been just another speaker without appeal, rather than a character whose memory is revered throughout the country." Applying this to Bob Wills and "San Antonio Rose" Milsten concluded, "I think this explains what you [Bornstein] had in mind when you talked about 'that certain something.' "

The persistence of Bob Wills and the eloquent arguments of David Randolph Milsten finally brought the results they wanted. On November 22, 1940, Saul H. Bornstein wrote Milsten: "We have gone back to the original lyrics and the original composition as given to us, per your request. . . . Columbia Record Co. has given it to Dick Jurgens and also Les Brown, and one will record it. The Victor Company has submitted it to Larry Clinton. . . ." Bob Wills and Milsten won the battle over which version of "San Antonio Rose" would be published, but both Wills and Irving Berlin won the war.[15]

To save face and further confusion, the Berlin firm published the composition, the way Bob originally wrote it, as "New San Antonio Rose." This title not only distinguished it from the firm's revision, but the printed version now also had the same name, music, and lyrics as the million-seller recording Wills made in April 1940. The Berlin firm had to recall all the copies of their revised editions and replace thousands of them with "New San Antonio Rose." The company never again tried to "correct" the music of Bob Wills.

Wills' recording of "New San Antonio Rose" was by no means the only successful recording of the song. After the music was published in its original form, several artists recorded it. Bing Crosby's "New San Antonio Rose" was released the end of January 1941 and sold more than 84,500 discs the last three days of the month. Eventually, it sold more than one-and-a-half million copies and won Crosby his second gold record. Bob Wills always believed that Crosby's recording of "New San Antonio Rose" was the turning point in his own career; it played a large role in changing his image from that of a provincial Southwesterner to that of a national and even international musical figure. Whether Wills overemphasized the importance of the Crosby recording and underemphasized his own is debatable. One thing is certain: both Wills and Crosby profited from "New San Antonio Rose." The song was so popular in 1942 that Bob Wills and his Texas Playboys recorded it with Crosby near the eighteenth green at Southern Hills Country

Bob Wills hollering while Tommy Duncan sings (one of the few photographs in which Wills is hollering or talking to a member of the band), 1940 or 1941 (*Reproduced by permission of Wymouth Young, KVOO Tulsa*)

Bob Wills and his orchestra in 1940. *Front row, left to right*: Leon McAuliffe, Bob Wills, Jesse Ashlock, Eldon Shamblin; *second row*: Herman Arnspiger, Zeb McNally, Joe Ferguson, Tiny Mott, Johnnie Lee Wills, Tommy Duncan, Al Stricklin, O. W. Mayo; *back row*: Everett Stover, Tubby Lewis, Smokey Dacus, Son Lansford. (*Reprinted by permission from Townsend*, San Antonio Rose)

Club in Tulsa, then offered to give a copy to the person buying the most war bonds. Leon McAuliffe reported that someone bought $250,000 in bonds to get that limited edition of "New San Antonio Rose."[16]

World War II played a large role in introducing Wills' music to foreign audiences. Servicemen took his records with them, and many sang his songs on aircraft carriers and in foxholes around the world. A letter from two servicemen in Germany, however, indicates that Wills' music was probably known to Germans before the Yanks got there. "While tossin' some Jerries out of a house we ran onto some old records and among them we were surprised to find some of your records—Rose of San Antonio," they wrote. "We would like to have you play a song for our wives. . . . How about 'Deep in the Heart of Texas'—because we are sure as hell deep in the heart of Germany."[17]

Not only did servicemen take Bob Wills' famous songs with them, they also took his famous holler. Especially after his recording of "New San Antonio Rose," Bob Wills hollers and expressions became an international trademark. His greatest popularity came on the eve of and during World War II, at just the right time for servicemen to take his music and his folk expressions around the world. Many jokes derived from these, some of them downright pornographic. One incident concerned British and American pilots in England training for combat. The leader of the British squadron, as a signal to the other British pilots that he was beginning to go into his maneuver, called, "Tally Ho!" Both the British and the Yankee pilots picked up his expression on their radios. When the Yanks were ready to follow the maneuver, their leader turned his aircraft and shouted in Bob Wills fashion, "Ah haa!" Servicemen have told me of meeting other Americans, especially Texans, during World War II, in the jungles of the Pacific, the deserts of Africa, on the snow-covered battlefields of Germany, and receiving a welcomed greeting of "Ah haa, San Antone."[18]

From 1940 to 1948, Bob Wills enjoyed great financial and artistic success. He made nearly twenty films in Hollywood, recorded many big-selling records, and drew crowds as large as any dance orchestra in American history. World War II marked the beginning of the end of the success that Bob and other band leaders had, by then, taken for granted. After 1950, people would never again go in great numbers to the hotel ballrooms and other dance establishments. Television and other changes in American entertainment habits produced an American who sat passively before the television or rock and roll groups or country western bands merely to listen, not to dance. This brought an end to one of the greatest ages in American music—the

Age of Swing. Big orchestras like Tommy Dorsey's and western swing bands like Bob Wills' played dance music and depended on dancers for their livelihood. By 1950, the age was ending and so was the dance bonanza that had gone on since the early thirties.

Like other big dance bands, Wills' popularity declined. Though the heyday of his career was over by 1950, Bob continued to draw good crowds and make successful recordings until a stroke forced his retirement in 1969. Throughout his career his most-requested song was "New San Antonio Rose." His musicians used to gamble on how many times the band would have to play it at an engagement—ten, fifteen, or how many times![19] By the mid-forties the song was so well known that the "New" was dropped, and it became known as "San Antonio Rose" whether it was played as an instrumental or with lyrics.

It will soon be fifty years since Wills recorded the original melody, and bands, popular orchestras, symphony orchestras, and artists of various kinds still play and record "San Antonio Rose." In March 1971, it was still available on forty-five different records by thirty-eight different artists, from Arthur Fiedler and the Boston Pops to a rock arrangement by the Ventures.[20] Fiedler liked the song so well, he released it on at least three different albums. The best I could determine from looking at recording data in 1975 at Bourne Music Company (successor to Irving Berlin, Incorporated), more than four hundred recordings had been made of the song. More recordings were made of it in 1974 than in 1954. This was due largely to the revival of interest in both Wills and western swing. For example, Wills' last recordings, made in late 1973, outsold every other album in his entire career, and in 1975, the National Academy of Recording Arts and Sciences gave it the recording industry's highest honor, a Grammy Award. In 1980, Willie Nelson and Ray Price recorded a very successful tribute album that not only included the song but was named "San Antonio Rose." Bing Crosby sang the "Rose of San Antone," as he called it, on the television show in which he was honored on his fiftieth anniversary as a recording star. In 1982, Clint Eastwood employed some of Bob Wills' Texas Playboys to perform "San Antonio Rose" and Johnny Gimble to play Bob Wills in a segment of his movie, *Honky Tonk Man*.

Nearly thirty years after "San Antonio Rose" was recorded, it was sung before the largest audience in its history. People around the world listened as astronauts Charles Conrad and Alan Bean serenaded them with two songs from outer space and Apollo 12—one of them "San Antonio Rose." [21]

Fortune appears to have smiled on "San Antonio Rose" throughout its history. Survival in New Mexico, in 1928, practically forced Wills to write the original music. When he rearranged the music for recording in 1938, Arthur Satherley named it "San Antonio Rose." In 1940, Irving Berlin compelled Wills to add the lyrics that played such an important role in the success of the song. The *name* of the song was so fortuitous. I wonder if it would have been nearly as popular had it lacked that romantic title, "San Antonio Rose." Think of the outcome had Satherley called it "Detroit Rose" or "Pittsburgh Rose" or "Des Moines Rose." I cannot believe the song would have lived beyond its first birthday had the lyrics read:

> Deep within my heart lies a melody
> A song of Old Houston
> Where in dreams I live beside the Astrodome

Historian Joe Frantz remarked: "Bob Wills deserves to be remembered in American culture for writing 'San Antonio Rose.' Wherever I go, Germany or England or South America, and they sing American songs, 'San Antonio Rose' is one they always sing." The song has a much higher place in American culture than just the run-of-the-mill song that is popular one year and forgotten the next. "San Antonio Rose" has reached a place where it has become a part of Americana. In Texas, where the music was born, it has entered the folklore of the people. So has Bob's famous holler that accompanied the 1940 recording. A scholar of Texas culture and folklore recently wrote that Texans often greet each other with "Ah haa, San Antone." Other Texans who feel exceptionally good and want to let people know they are real Lone Star Staters give out with Bob's famous holler, "Ah haa, San Antone."

This famous holler is a good example of how folk expressions, folklore, and folk legends originate. In neither "San Antonio Rose" (1938) nor "New San Antonio Rose" (1940) did Bob Wills say, "Ah haa, San Antone." In 1938, he said, "Ah haa, Leon" and later, "Oh! That San Antonio Rose, Yes!" In 1940 he said, "Ah haa, my San Antonio Rose." In both these cases, he pronounced distinctly "San Antonio." After Tommy Duncan sang the part of the lyrics that read "a song of old San Antone," Bob hollered repeating only his last two words: "SAN ANTONE." Almost immediately throughout the country people went about the streets and in dance establishments hollering, "Ah haa, San Antone." No one, I ever heard, said, "Ah haa, my San Antonio Rose" or "Ah haa, San Antonio." Neither the folk nor Bob said "San Antonio," unless they "were putting on airs." People put Bob's first "Ah haa" with his second holler "San Antone" and created the folk expression, "Ah haa, San Antone." Later Bob evidently thought that was the way he did it in 1940, so he, too, began hollering, "Ah haa, San Antone."

When the people saw him in person for the first time, they wanted to hear Bob Wills cry out "Ah haa, that San Antone Rose" or even better "Ah haa, San Antone." They usually smiled and sometimes hollered with him or back to him or to each other. Bob's hollering was inspiring to his musicians; it also had a way of picking up the audience, calling them to attention, and bringing life and happiness to those on the dance floor. One might like or dislike Wills, but no one could ignore him when he hollered. The fans found it honest and appealing; they found in Wills a freedom that most people wish to possess and express, but for various reasons suppress. More formal, straightlaced, and inhibited musicians laughed at what they thought were crude antics. Ironically, most of those musicians are forgotten, and the people made a legend, a folk hero of Bob Wills.[22]

A college student from Colorado asked me recently: "Dr. Townsend, what does 'Ah haa San Antonio' mean? What is the origin of that expression?" What a golden opportunity that was for me to tell him the story I have just told in this essay, the story of "old Doc Garner's favorite fiddle tune," my favorite song, and Jim Rob Wills, whose biography is summed up in the first lines of his "San Antonio Rose," the words that are both his figurative and literal epitaph:

> Deep within my heart lies a melody.
> A song of old San Antone.

There *was* a melody in his soul, and many are glad he expressed it in that song about the rose of San Antone.

Notes

1. Much of the source material for this essay is based on the research I have done during the last decade and a half on Wills and his music. For more detailed footnotes and documentation see Charles R. Townsend, *San Antonio Rose: The Life and Music of Bob Wills* (Urbana: University of Illinois Press, 1976), especially "Essay on Sources," 325-35.
2. Interviews: Bob Wills, Ruby Wills Sullivan, Eloise Wills House, Edna Wills; see also Ruth Sheldon, *'Hubbin' It: The Life of Bob Wills* (Tulsa: Privately published, 1938), 69-72.

3. *Ethnomusicology* 14 (January 1970): 105; and *Chicken Scratch: Popular Dance Music of the Indians of Southern Arizona*, Canyon Records, C-6085.
4. Interview: Bob Wills; Edna Wills, "What I Know About 'Bob Wills'" (November 1972). Edna Wills was Bob's first wife, and when she learned I was writing his biography, she wrote down her reflections on their life together and gave the manuscript to me when I interviewed her. Interviews: Harold Ham, Mrs. F. O. Ham, Jewel Hardaway, John Luther Garner, Laverne Simmons Barnhill.
5. Interviews: Bob Wills, Herman Arnspiger, Durwood Brown.
6. Interviews: Bob Wills, Arthur Satherley, Leon McAuliffe; see "The Bob Wills Recordings: A Comprehensive Discography" in Townsend, *Life and Music of Bob Wills*, 337-76.
7. Interviews: Bob Wills, Arthur Satherley, Johnnie Lee Wills, Smokey Dacus, Al Stricklin; *Downbeat* 4 (January 1937): 15. See also letter from Chuck Suber of *Downbeat* to Charles R. Townsend, July 2, 1973.
8. Interviews: O. W. Mayo, Wayne Johnson, Bob Wills.
9. Interviews: Eldon Shamblin, Leon McAuliffe, O. W. Mayo, Bob Wills, Al Stricklin, Sleepy Johnson, Johnnie Lee Wills.
10. Townsend, *Life and Music of Bob Wills*, 344-45.
11. Interviews: Bob Wills, Leon McAuliffe.
12. Interviews: Smokey Dacus, Bob Wills, Johnnie Lee Wills.
13. Interview: Bob Wills.
14. A list of gold record awards was researched and prepared in August 1967 by Columbia Records (CBS Records Division), New York. I am grateful to Martine McCarthy for making this list available.
15. Letters from David Randolph Milsten to Saul Bornstein, July 16, 1940, August 13, 1940; Bornstein to Milsten, August 9, 1940, November 22, 1940. Interviews: David Randolph Milsten, O. W. Mayo, Bob Wills.
16. *Bing: A Musical Autobiography*, Decca DX-151, pp. 15, 18; interviews: Leon McAuliffe, Harry Rassmussin, Bob Wills.
17. Letter from James Fletcher and Harry D. Dye to Bob Wills, April 27, 1945.
18. Townsend, *Life and Music of Bob Wills*, 106-8, 106 note 63.
19. Interviews: Al Stricklin, Eldon Shamblin, Smokey Dacus, Johnny Gimble, Glenn Rhees, Bob Wills, Betty Wills Sheets.
20. *Phonolog Reports*, March 1, 1971, pp. 118-9A-9B.
21. "Country Music from Outer Space," *CMA Close Up* 11 (December 1969): 1.
22. Interviews: Smokey Dacus, Al Stricklin, Bob Wills, Johnnie Lee Wills, Betty Wills Sheets, Eldon Shamblin.

"The Cowboys' Christmas Ball"

THE HISTORICITY OF A COWBOY BALLAD

by Connie Ricci

When we think of folk songs, cowboy ballads—or at least songs related to the frontier—are often the first to tug at our imaginations, provoking delightful notions of those bygone "good ole days." In his many years of dedicated collecting of this element of America's oral tradition, John Lomax discovered a multiplicity of ballads which range over most aspects of the cowboy's daily existence: his work, his play, his isolation, and his communal endeavors. In his book *Cowboy Songs and Other Frontier Ballads*, Lomax included a ballad, "The Cowboys' Christmas Ball," that not only frolics with the imagination but also provides an account of the history of this particular event, thereby preserving an authentic rendition of those "good ole days."[1]

Interestingly enough, it should be noted that this ballad that Lomax collected from the oral tradition was first written as a poem by William Lawrence Chittenden. Chittenden wrote the poem in honor of an actual cowboy hoedown held on December 24, 1885, at the Star Hotel in Anson, Texas. M. G. Rhoads, proprietor of the Star Hotel, often sponsored get-togethers for the ranchers and their families, according to Mrs. Keene, Rhoads' daughter. His idea for the Christmas ball, one of which was given in honor of a young cowhand's marriage, proved to be so popular that it became an annual event which traditionally honored the year's newlyweds.[2]

Chittenden's recording of this event is of special interest because it documents a significant cross section of those early-day pioneers involved in the settling of West Texas. In this rendition we also see evidence of the importance of play and communal activities to those early settlers, for many came from faraway counties just to attend Rhoads' ball.

Fittingly, the first person mentioned in the ballad is Hec McCann (McEachin), who edited the Anson newspaper, the *Texas Western*, and first published Chittenden's poem in his paper on June 19, 1890.[3] Next mentioned is Frank Smith, who, with his brother, organized the first bank in Anson. Smith was well known for his tall tales and yarns, and his death in 1917 was a loss to the community.[4]

Following Smith, John Milsap and the Widow Wall are indicated to have been among those present. Although information concerning Mrs. Wall is not available, it is probable that she was a local resident. Milsap, on the other hand, was well known for his hunting skills and his reputation gained as a sheriff in Paris, Texas. He settled in Anson in 1887 and died there in 1926.[5]

The famous "Windy Bill" cited in the ballad is William Wilkinson. He worked as a ranch hand for the Swenson Ranch before moving to Sterling City where he passed away. Besides calling the dances, "Windy" acted as book-keeper. Since the men outnumbered the women considerably, it was Windy's job to keep count of how many dances each man danced in order that all of the men might have an equal chance of getting onto the dance floor.[6]

Others included in the ballad are: Spur Treadwell, a pioneer druggist from Dallas; Cross P. Charley's bride, Mrs. Charley P'Pool of Haskell (Cross P was the P'Pool brand); T-Diamond, Senator W. J. Bryan, so nicknamed for his T-Diamond spread north of Anson; Big Boston, an Anson businessman named Mr. Foster; T-Bar Dick, foreman of T-Bar Ranch (no one recalled his real name or what finally became of him); McAllister (no information); Varn Andrews, one of Anson's first two doctors; Doc Hollis, a pioneer physician who is credited by the American Medical Association as having performed the first appendectomy in the United States; and Little Pitchfork, a rancher from the Guthrie area.[7]

That Chittenden used poetic license by naming among these people some who were not at the scene of the original ball detracts none from the historical validity of his creation.[8] Most likely a synthesis of several years' attendance at this annual festivity, the poem's value lies in the fact that in it Chittenden preserved for future generations a scene truly reflective of the frontier West. His poem, packed with its ranchers, newspapermen, politicians, doctors, sheriffs, cowhands, and ladies—not to mention its twangy West Texas dialect and regional allusions—vividly recreates a slice of West Texas history.

Although perhaps ironical, it is nonetheless appropriate that this rendition of West Texas history came from one who was a "foreigner" to the Southwest. Such was certainly Larry Chittenden.

Born in Montclair, New Jersey, on March 23, 1862, to Henry and Henrietta Chittenden, William Lawrence Chittenden came from a prestigious, well-established New England family which traced its ancestry back to William Chittenden of Kent, England. Chittenden's father, Henry, was a successful New York merchant, a learned Bible student, and one of the founders of Plymouth Church. Also adding to the distinction of the family was Chittenden's uncle, Simeon B. Chittenden, a congressman from Brooklyn.[9]

Larry Chittenden began his career as a reporter for the *New York Times*. In 1883, he left New England and came to Texas, where he traveled as a dry-goods salesman and a news correspondent. It was during this time that Simeon Chittenden asked his nephew to inspect some property he had purchased in Jones County, Texas. Consequently, on December 24, 1885, Chittenden, on this trip to inspect his uncle's ranching interests, arrived at Anson, Texas, in time to view Rhoads' Christmas ball. Two years later, Chittenden moved to Jones County where he took up ranching for awhile. Although he never became a true rancher, Chittenden attempted to capture the essence of ranch life in his poetry. From that attempt to recreate the western element came Chittenden's poem, "The Cowboys' Christmas Ball." [10]

Though first seen in print, the appeal of "The Cowboys' Christmas Ball" was such that it soon found its way into the oral tradition from which John Lomax collected it. And whether remembered as a poem written by Larry Chittenden or as a cowboy ballad collected by John Lomax, "The Cowboys' Christmas Ball" is significant culturally because it provides an authentic reflection of the tradition and spirit of the West Texas region and its inhabitants during the era of the cowboy.

THE COWBOYS' CHRISTMAS BALL

Way out in western Texas, where the Clear Fork's waters flow,
Where the cattle are a-browsin' and the Spanish ponies grow;
Where the Northers come a-whistlin' from beyond the Neutral Strip;
And the prairie dogs are sneezin', as though they had the grip;

Where the coyotes come a-howlin' round the ranches after dark,
And the mockin' birds are singin' to the lovely medder lark;
Where the 'possum and the badger and the rattlesnakes abound,
And the monstrous stars are winkin' o'er a wilderness profound;

Where lonesome, tawny prairies melt into airy streams,
While the Double Mountains slumber in heavenly kinds of dreams;
Where the antelope is grazin' and the lonely plovers call—
It was there I attended the Cowboys' Christmas Ball.

The town was Anson City, old Jones' county seat,
Where they raised Polled Angus cattle and waving whiskered wheat;
Where the air is soft and bammy and dry and full of health,
Where the prairies is explodin' with agricultural wealth;

Where they print the *Texas Western*, that Hec McCann supplies
With news and yarns and stories, of most amazing size;
Where Frank Smith "pulls the badger" on knowing tenderfeet;
And Democracy's triumphant and mighty hard to beat;

Where lives that good old hunter, John Milsap from Lamar,
Who used to be the sheriff "back east in Paris, sah"!
'Twas there, I say, at Anson with the lovely Widder Wall,
That I went to that reception, the Cowboys' Christmas Ball.

The boys had left the ranches and come to town in piles;
The ladies, kinder scatterin', had gathered in for miles.
And yet the place was crowded, as I remember well,
'Twas gave on this occasion at the Morning Star Hotel.

The music was a fiddle and a lively tambourine,
And a viol came imported, by the stage from Abilene.
The room was togged out gorgeous—with mistletoe and shawls,
And the candles flickered festious, around the airy walls.

The wimmen folks looked lovely—the boys looked kinder treed,
Till the leader commenced yelling, "Whoa, fellers, let's stampede,"
And the music started sighing and a-wailing through the hall
As a kind of introduction to the Cowboys' Christmas Ball.

The leader was a feller that came from Swenson's ranch—
They called him Windy Billy from Little Deadman's Branch.
His rig was kinder keerless—big spurs and high-heeled boots;
He had the reputation that comes when fellers shoots.

His voice was like the bugle upon the mountain height;
His feet were animated, and a mighty movin' sight,
When he commenced to holler, "Now, fellers, shake your pen!
Lock horns ter all them heifers and rustle them like men;

"Saloot yer lovely critters; neow swing and let 'em go;
Climb the grapevine round 'em; neow ali hands do-ce-do!
You maverick, jine the round-up—jes' skip the waterfall,"
Huh! Hit was getting active, the Cowboys' Christmas Ball.

The boys was tolerable skittish, the ladies powerful neat,
That old bass viol's music just got there with both feet!
That wailin', frisky fiddle, I never shall forget;
And Windy kept a-singin'—I think I hear him yet—

"Oh, X's, chase yer squirrels, and cut 'em to our side;
Spur Treadwell to the center, with Cross P Charley's bride,
Doc Hollis down the center, and twine the ladies' chain,
Van Andrews, pen the fillies in big T Diamond's train.

"All pull your freight together, neow swallow fork and change;
Big Boston, lead the trail herd through little Pitchfork's range.
Purr round yer gentle pussies, neow rope and balance all!"
Huh! Hit were gettin' active—the Cowboys' Christmas Ball.

The dust riz fast and furious; we all jes' galloped 'round,
Till the scenery got so giddy that T Bar Dick was drowned.
We buckled to our partners and told 'em to hold on,
Then shook our hoofs like lightning until the early dawn.

Don't tell me 'bout cotillions or germans. No, sir-ee!
That whirl at Anson City jes' takes the cake with me.
I'm sick of lazy shufflin's, of them I've had my fill,
Give me a frontier breakdown backed up by Windy Bill.

McAllister ain't nowhere, when Windy leads the show;
I've seen 'em both in harness and so I ought ter know.
Oh, Bill, I shan't forget yer, and I oftentimes recall
That lively gaited sworray—the Cowboys' Christmas Ball.

Notes

1. John A. Lomax and Alan Lomax, *Cowboy Songs and Other Frontier Ballads* (London: Macmillan Company, 1938), 246-49.

2. "Second Re-Enactment of Famous Ball Attracts Many," *Western Enterprise*, December 26, 1935; "Colorful Cowboys' Christmas Ball Inaugurated 53 Years Ago," *Abilene Reporter News*, December 18, 1938; "Original Ball and Star Hotel Are Described by 'Eye Witness,'" *Western Observer*, December 16, 1954. There is some variance in opinion as to the actual date of the original ball.

3. "Second Re-Enactment"; Larry Chittenden; "The Cowboys' Christmas Ball," *Texas Western*, June 19, 1890 (reprinted in *That Lively Gaited Sworray*, Cowboy Christmas Ball Association, 1946, p.4).

4. "Second Re-Enactment."

5. "Second Re-Enactment."

6. Leonora Barrett, "The Story of Folk Dancing at the Chittenden Cowboys' Christmas Ball," *Southwestern Musician* (September-October 1943): 19.

7. "Chittenden Ranch House Is Located Near Water Well," *Western Observer*, December 16, 1954; "Second Re-Enactment"; Garford Wilkinson, "The First Cowboys' Christmas Ball," *Quarter Horse Journal* (December 1960): 20.

8. "Colorful Cowboys' Christmas Ball," 10.

9. "Chittenden, William L.," *Who Was Who In America*, Vol. 1, 1897–1942, p. 218; *Montclair–Glen Ridge Bulletin*, November 8, 1930.

10. Wilkinson, "First Cowboys' Christmas Ball," 21; "The Cowboys' Christmas Ball," *Farm and Ranch* 55 (February 15, 1934): 2; Leonora Barrett, "The Story of Folk Dancing," 19-22; "W. F. Flynt Tells How Chittenden Enjoyed Ranch," *Western Observer*, December 16, 1954.

THE COWBOYS' CHRISTMAS BALL

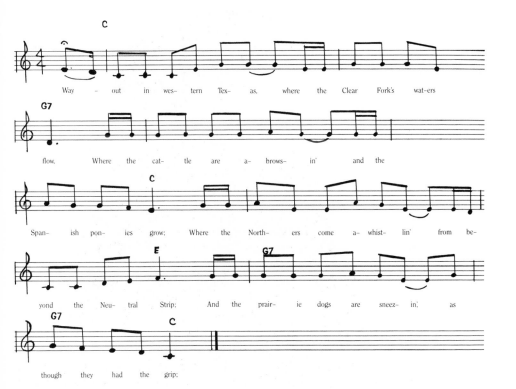

Way – out in wes- tern Tex- as, where the Clear Fork's wat-ers flow, Where the cat- tle are a- brows- in' and the Span- ish pon- ies grow; Where the North- ers come a- whist- lin' from be- yond the Neu- tral Strip; And the prair- ie dogs are sneez- in', as though they had the grip;

Mexican vaquero (*Reproduced by permission of Bill Wittliff*)

Three Corridos of the Big Bend

by Elton Miles

A tale of murder, accidental death, or cowboy life in early days of the Big Bend sometimes was put in the form of a local Mexican-American ballad, or *corrido*. These subjects are typical of such ballads, though the best known deal with border conflict, border outlaws, and Mexican-Americans defending their rights against oppressive lawmen, American or Mexican. Hence, the most renowned probably is "El Corrido de Gregorio Cortez," memorialized in the book by Américo Paredes and in a motion picture for public television. Even so, the earliest known to Paredes, "El Corrido de Kansas," dating from the 1860s, tells of the death of a South Texas vaquero, slain by a steer on a cattle drive, and of the foreman's reporting the tragedy to the boy's mother.

Such a tragedy and the reporting of it make up three *corridos* of the Big Bend.[1] Like all indigenous ballads, these are truly songs of the people, songs about real persons and events, usually sad. They were sung within and for the local Mexican-American population at private parties or in late evening cow camps when the day's work was done. In function, aside from entertainment, they are a modern survival of the old-time minstrel's entuned reporting of news that does not seem to grow old with singing it over and again.

In a sense these three *corridos* have survived as folk poetry rather than as song. In each instance somebody remembered the words, but not the tune. Having originated on the Texas-Mexican border in mid-nineteenth century, the folk composition and singing of the *corrido* began its rapid decline in the 1930s.[2] While the phonograph record preserved many a *corrido*, it also replaced the live local composer and singer. None of these songs dates later than the early Thirties. Nowadays, almost every new *corrido* is the

37

product of professional musicians and is purveyed by disc recordings over the air used by the "Spanish Hour" of Southwestern radio stations. A recent *corrido* that earned brief popularity tells of a shooting spree during a San Antonio festival parade in 1979. Reportedly, the record's first pressing sold out on the day of its release.

In these *corridos* from the Big Bend, two methods of composition are seen, both typical of balladry and folk poetry in general. "El Corrido del Rancho Jandred-huan" is said to have resulted from communal composition by several cowboys inspired by a habitual rhymemaker among them. The other two seem to have been composed each by one person, his identity not specified in the song. As for the man who wrote about the death of Antonio Casas, however, his name is remembered in the town where he lived.

El Corrido de Antonio Casas

This story of sudden murder on drunken impulse in a friendly setting occurred in Alpine in 1908 in a bar owned by one "Mocho," a local nickname for a one-armed person (or with a leg or even a finger missing). Mocho's cantina was located in the vicinity of Avenue F and 7th Street, where the Casas family owned property. The barbershop of Julián Ramírez now stands on that corner where the murder is said to have happened. Salomón Ramos believes that a stanza is missing from this version, lines suggesting that mere drunkenness caused the shooting. He remembers only one line of the missing part: "Por los tragos que tomaron. . . ." (Because of the liquor they had drunk . . . .) At that time the Brewster County Sheriff was J. Allen Walton, and there were several physicians in Alpine. Juan Gallegos later worked in the 1940s in the Brewster County Court House for Sheriff Clarence Hord, and in the Fifties owned an Alpine beer-bar called "The Bull." He is father of Brewster County Commissioner Ernest Gallego.

According to Salomón, Juan Vega is the author of this *corrido*. A well educated and cultured man, Juan Vega established the Amor Trabajo Unión Club (Love-Work-Unity) in Alpine as a respectable social club for Mexican-American citizens. Having lost its original purpose, the ATU Club is now a privately owned bar, and none of Juan Vega's family live in Alpine.

EL CORRIDO DE ANTONIO CASAS

| En mil novecientos ocho | In nineteen hundred and eight |
| Antonio Casas murió, | Antonio Casas died |

En la cantina del Mocho—	In Mocho's bar—
Un cobarde lo mató.	A coward killed him.
Hicieron contribución	They all chipped in
Para comprar la bebida;	To buy the drinks;
Valido de la ocacion	Taking advantage of that occasion,
El otro le quitó la vida.	The other took his life.
Estaban tomando café,	They were drinking coffee,
Le disparó dos balazos;	He fired two shots at him;
Uno de ellos fue el que	One of those was that
Le hizo la alma pedasos.	Which splintered his soul.
Ay viene alburiendo el día	Here comes the morning
Dando luz y resplandor	Bringing light and brightness,
Para que fueran a traer	So they could go and bring
El cherife y el doctor.	The sheriff and the doctor.
El cherife y Juan Gallegos	The sheriff and Juan Gallegos
Hicieron muy buenas trazas,	Made a good plan,
Que dicen a Juan Vega	They told Juan Vega
Que diera aviso a las Casas.	To go tell the Casas.
En el mundo se navega,	In the world one moves around,
Y en la tumba se descansa.	In the grave one rests.
Esto le dije a Juan Vega	That's what I told Juan Vega,
Que dispense la confianza.	May he excuse my confiding in him.
La mujer de Antonio Casas	The wife of Antonio Casas
Goza de un sueño profundo,	Is in a deep sleep
Sin saber que Antonio Casas	Without knowing that Antonio Casas
Gozaba del otro mundo	Has passed on to the other world.
Ya con esta me despido	With this I bid farewell,
Dandola vuelta a una casa.	Turning the thing over in my mind.
Aquí se acaba el corrido	This is the end of the *corrido*
Del Señor Antonio Casas.	Of Señor Antonio Casas.

In the Alpine barbershop of Salomón Ramos, we were talking about the two following *corridos*, when elderly José Luna said he knew one too. In a few days' time a friend had written out the above ballad at his dictation. It was delivered to me by "Terry" Martinez early in May 1981.

El Corrido De José Martinez

This ballad tells of the accidental death of an expert cowboy and rider, José Martinez, in about 1915. The incident deserved a *corrido*, because it was not only shocking but ironic for such a skilled rider to be killed by being thrown from a horse. At the time of the accident José Martinez was working at a part-time job on Las Peñas Ranch, near Casa Piedra in southern Presidio County. Working with him at the moment was his good friend, a man called Séledonio. It was he who brought the sad news to the nearest neighbors on El Alamito Ranch, which was owned by a Herrera family. José's regular, full-time employment was on Jim P. Wilson's Green Valley Ranch, also in southern Presidio County and south of the 02 Ranch.

EL CORRIDO DE JOSÉ MARTINEZ

El día quince de septiembre,	It was the fifteenth of September,
Presente lo tengo yo,	I remember it well,
En el Rancho de Las Peñas	On the Las Peñas Ranch
José Martinez murio.	José Martinez died.
Seledonio se llamaba	Seledonio was the name
El que andaba con	Of the one who went around with
José,	José;
Fue el que vino a traer la nueva	It was he who came to bring the news
Lo que a José le pasaba.	Of what had happened to José.
Esa gente de El Alamito	Those people of El Alamito
Fue la que ayudó a	Were the ones who helped in the
velarlo,	all-night vigil,
Otro día por la mañana	The next morning
Llevaron a sepultarlo.	They took him out to bury him.
En el Rancho de Grin Vali	On the Green Valley Ranch,
Donde trabajaba el hombre,	Where the man worked,

Veinte años tenía en el oficio	Twenty years he had been in the trade
Y nunca lo habian tumbado.	And he had never been thrown.

—Ahora sí, compañeritos,	Well now, friends,
Ya me encuentro bajo de tierra.	I find myself under the ground.
Ay les dejo de memoria	I left as remembrances
Cuarta, montura, y espuela.	My quirt, saddle, and spurs.

The words of this *corrido* are as remembered in 1979 by Salomón Ramos, a "stove up" lifelong vaquero, whose broken bones do not allow him to ride much anymore. He is constable and part-time barber in Alpine, and he raises fighting-chickens. Salomón says that in about 1973 he was surprised to hear a recording of "El Corrido de José Martinez" played on the Spanish Hour of Alpine Radio Station KVLF. He said, "I didn't think anybody but some of the old cowboys knew it." Spanish Hour Director Vic Torres does not remember such a record, and KVLF does not now have such a record in their files.

It was Salomón's brother who recovered the next *corrido*.

El Corrido del Rancho Jandred-huan

The events in this song occurred in 1931 over a period of at least two days during a roundup (*corrida, rodeo*) on the 101 Ranch in Brewster County, southwest of Alpine. The event in the third stanza from the end, however, took place somewhat later on the adjoining 02 Ranch. At that time the 101 belonged to Mrs. Iva Guthrie Turney and the 02 to her husband, W. W. Turney, both then of El Paso and formerly of Alpine.[3]

Salomón Ramos, the thirteen-year-old near the end of the song and still called "Mon," says each man had about five horses assigned to him, they were all hard to catch, and the cowboys "made the *corrido* because the horses all pitched." Yet, he observed that the song is really about El Moro, "one of the famous horses around here," and at that time one of the worst to buck. He also said that this roundup on the 101 was conducted by the crew from the 02 in a husband-wife business arrangement.

The words were obtained in 1973 from Leonardo Pando by Alfonso Ramos (Salomón's brother). Leonardo, with bushy mustachio and big black hat aslant, was still a working cowboy in his last days on the J. D. Holman Ranch east of Alpine in the late 1970s.

Above: Vaquero on bronco; *below*: Vaquero with Anglo caporal branding a horse (*Reproduced by permission of the Archives of the Big Bend, Sul Ross State University*)

I asked Salomón if the song is supposed to be funny, and he said, "No. It's just about what happened." Pando told Alfonso Ramos that as the 101 roundup progressed over several days, most of the stanzas were composed by Leonides Valenzuela, though some were made by other men on the job. Here, then, is an account of the communal composition of a folksong, the informal lead taken by an acknowledged sort of "minstrel." Called *poeta y vaquero* in the ballad, Leonides is remembered by Salomón as often reciting verses he had invented. Reflecting the Great Depression days (and using a localism, *relís*) one goes like this:

Vuela, vuela, palomito,	Fly, fly, little dove,
Párate en aquel relís,	Stop on that cliff,
Anda visa a los de pueblo	Go on and tell those in town
Que ya se acabo el Relif.	That there's no more Relief.

Meaning "relief money." Leonides became a carpenter and moved to Carlsbad, New Mexico, where he died.

Chonito Luján is the first cowboy El Moro pitches off in the song. Though his new bride, Amelia, is distressed, Chonito was not permanently injured. Their daughter, Enedina Gallego Luján, later was married to the Brewster County Memorial Hospital administrator, Bill Donahoo. Now Amelia Gallego Cedillo, Amelia lives in Alpine. Chonito lives on a ranch he owns near San Carlos, Mexico, south of Lajitas, Texas.

The *caporal*—or foreman—was Dick Riddle, who died in Alpine some years ago. Secundo Franco, from Terlingua, was drowned some years past in the Rio Grande. Nicacio Ramírez worked as a top cowboy for Herbert Kokernot on the 06 Ranch north of Alpine. He was widely known as an expert roper and heeler in steer roping.

Old vaqueros remember El Moro and other horses almost as well as they do the people. While talking about this *corrido*, Salomón Ramos and former cowboy and ranch-cook Juan Valenzuela, who worked for Brewster County rancher Neville Haines, traced the later history of El Moro and other memorable horses. In the song, El Moro, a large gray, is also called El Ingrato— ungrateful, or terrible—as well as El Numero Uno. This horse died several years after the roundup when Juan Valenzuela was working him to a fresno, scraping out and cleaning a stock-tank. El Moro fell in the tank and was drowned.

Of the other horses mentioned in the song, El Morito became one of Leonardo Pando's favorite working horses. El Pinto, or "Paint," incidentally gives foreman Dick Riddle a bad time at the end of the song.

The lines of this *corrido* were recited in 1973 by Leonardo Pando to Alfonso Ramos, who wrote them down. Pando said that there are other versions, but that this is the original version which was formed during the roundup it deals with. He also said that some singers had made up verses about themselves and pretended they took part in the action but that they had been left out of this version of the song.

EL CORRIDO DEL RANCHO JANDRED-HUAN

Tengan señores presente
Lo que pasó el treinta y uno
En esa corrida afamada
En el Rancho del Ciento Uno.

Remember, you men present,
What happened in 'thirty-one
At that famous roundup
On the One-O-One Ranch.

El día trece de julio,
Me acquerdo bien de ese día,
Tumbó un caballo a Chonito
Se lo quitó con t'uy silla.

The thirteenth day of July,
I remember that day well,
A horse pitched off Chonito,
Threw him saddle and all.

Decía Amelia Luján
Triste y desesperada,
—No es posible que quede
    yo sola,
Estando recien yo casada.

Amelia Luján said,
Sad and desperate,
"It's not possible I should be
    left alone,
Having been so recently married."

Les dijo Chonito Luján,
—No puedo ya trabajar.
Ahí está El Moro malvado
Pa'l que lo quiera montar.

Chonito Luján said,
"I can't work anymore.
There's that bad El Moro
For anyone who wants to mount him."

Leonides, poeta y vaquero,
Dice al caporal acercando,
—El que pueda al Moro montar
Es el primo, Leonardo Pando.

Leonides, poet and cowboy,
Says, approaching the foreman,
"The man who can mount El Moro
Is my cousin, Leonardo Pando."

Entonces manda Leonardo,
Mirando al Moro de lado,

Then Leonardo commands,
Looking at El Moro sideways,

—Arrimen ya la remuda
Y lasen ese Moro afamado.

"Bring the fresh horse
And rope that famous Moro."

El caporal les advierte,
—Cuidao con ese caballo.
Ese caballo se juega,
Ya se ha quitáo buenos gallos.

The foreman advised them,
"Be careful with that horse.
That horse is untrustworthy;
He has thrown some good 'roosters.' "

Leonardo al caporal le contesta,
Con su sombrero de lado,
—Si ese caballo me tumba
Dejo de trabajar yo el ganado.

Leonardo answers the foreman,
With his hat on at a slant,
"If that horse should throw me,
I'll stop working cattle."

El catorce por la mañana,
Tengo presente ese rato
Ese Secundino Franco
También jinetio al Ingrato

On the fourteenth in the morning,
I remember that moment
That Secundino Franco
Also tamed that "ungrateful."

También Leonides Valenzuela
En el caballo El Morito,
Como no usaba cuarta
Le daba con el sombrerito.

Also Leonides Valenzuela
On a horse called Little Gray,
As he didn't use a quirt,
He would hit him with his little hat.

Gritaba Nicacio Ramírez
En medio de la polvadera
—En el corral no es nada,
Lo bueno va a ser afuera.

Nicacio Ramírez yelled
In the middle of the dust,
"In the corral it is nothing!
The best show will be outside."

Como Nicasio Ramírez
Para lazar no había ninguno.
También se jugó bonito
En el caballo Número Uno.

As for Nicasio Ramírez
There wasn't anyone as good at roping.
He also played beautifully
On the horse Number One.

Mon Ramos en La Potranca
montado
Contemplaba al Moro indomable
Cumpliá él trece años de edad
Mirábalo con ganas de entrarle.

Mon Ramos, mounted on
The Filly,
Thought about the untamable Moro.
He had just turned thirteen years old
He watched with desire to ride him.

Por la tarde pararon el
rodeo,
Empezaron los rancheros a
cortar;

That afternoon they stopped the
roundup,
The ranch hands began to cut out
the stock;

Above: Brush-popping vaquero; *below*: Vaquero roping horses out of the remuda (*Reproduced by permission of Bill Wittliff*)

Allí se rifó bonito	There was a pretty scuffling
El Pinto y el caporal.	Between Paint and the foreman.
Ya con esto me despido,	Now with this I depart,
Brindándome un vaso	Toasting myself with a glass
de cham-pan.	of champagne.
Aquí se acaba el corrido	Here ends the *corrido*
Del Rancho Jandred-huan.	Of the Hundred-One Ranch.

These *corridos* are three of many that originated among working folk in the Big Bend, telling stories of real events that are worth retelling in song. Many others seem all but lost forever, long forgotten. One, for example, tells of the fatal shooting of a man in Presidio by a presumed friend, who allegedly was a gunman for Sheriff "Dud" Barker in Fort Stockton. Another tells of the killing of an Alpine man in Puerto Rico, a settlement in Mexico near the Rio Grande.

Salomón Ramos, now in his late sixties, has heard some of these *corridos* sung by friends many times during hours of relaxation. He heard "Antonio Casas" sung by a Mexican citizen in Ojinaga at a house party. "We were drinking *sotol* and eating *menudo*," he said. Mostly he heard them back in the 1930s and 40s, sung by vaqueros resting in cow camp after the day's work. "Nobody could have a guitar on the One-O-One," Salomón said. "We lived in the open and it would get busted." So they just sang.

Notes

1. For their generous help in the translation of these *corridos*, I am indebted especially to Professor Brent Jensen and also to Dr. Russell Goodyear, Dr. Raymond Wheat, and Mrs. Don Stafford. Thanks are also due to Teresa Martinez for her help to both José Luna and to me.
2. See Américo Paredes, *With His Pistol In His Hand: A Border Ballad and Its Hero* (Austin: University of Texas Press, 1958), 129-50; and Paredes, "The Mexican *Corrido*: Its Rise and Fall," in Mody C. Boatright, Wilson M. Hudson, and Allen Maxwell, eds., *Madstones and Twisters*, Publications of the Texas Folklore Society, No. XXVIII (Dallas: Southern Methodist University Press, 1958), 91-105.
3. Iva Guthrie Turney was a great-aunt of Woody Guthrie's father, and she figures in two of Woody Guthrie's books, as "Aunt Sarah" in *Bound for Glory* and as "Aunt Patsy Greenseed" in *Seeds of Man*, which has its setting in the Big Bend. Guthrie uses the 02 Ranch name but places it south of Study Butte on the Sam Nail Ranch property in southern Brewster County.

Cowboy and Gaucho Songs

A COMPARISON

by Lawrence Clayton and Rosita Chazarreta

Although they lived in two different hemispheres, the North American cowboy and the South American gaucho developed similar cattle-oriented cultures that have left unique and lasting impressions upon people even in lands far removed geographically from the areas of origin. One of the richest of their legacies is a body of folk songs depicting details of the life and work of the two groups. Since the principal focus of these two authentic folk types was much the same, it is not surprising that their songs bear a remarkable likeness in subject matter and in attitudes toward life, even though two quite distinct poetic traditions are involved—the Anglo-Irish and the Spanish. A brief review of the similarities in historical background seems worthwhile before looking at some of the texts themselves.

The cowboys lived and worked on the plains and in brush-choked regions that were largely arid and semi-arid. Similarly the gaucho roamed the Pampa, an extensive plain of some 250,000 square miles in the provinces of Buenos Aires, Santa Fe, Córdoba, and La Pampa, largely in the central part of Argentina. The ingredients that fostered the North American range cattle industry—ample grass and water—are present on the vast Pampa. The other ingredients came to Argentina when Spanish explorers brought horses in 1535 and cattle around 1575. By 1580, large herds of both horses and cattle roamed wild over the prairies of South America,[1] much as they did on the coastal plain of what is now Texas after the introduction in 1540 of Spanish cattle from Mexico. Horses, of course, had been introduced slightly earlier in Texas as the conquistadores moved northward out of Mexico in search of treasure to the north.[2]

Both cowboy and gaucho helped tame their plains, contending with hostile Indians, also mounted on the formerly wild horses, for the use of the territories. The South American Indians had quickly assimilated the horse into their culture. Since the bison was not present in South America as it was in North America, the South American Indians learned to depend upon the wild cattle as a diet staple and a marketable commodity. Herds were driven by some Indians to Chile for sale there, a curious parallel with the much-romanticized activity of the cowboy. When the Spanish demand for cattle for export of hides, tallow, and hair infringed upon the Indians' needs, the inevitable economic conflict erupted. When Argentina sought to establish its independence from Spain in the early 1800s, the gaucho became an important political and military force in the country, a role never assumed by the cowboy. Even though cowmen, landowners, and the like certainly figured heavily in the political development of the West in North America, there was no foreign power to overcome there; hence, the only civil conflict was the War between the States, fought largely outside the Southwest and before the burgeoning of the cattle kingdom.

The trappings of the cowboy were the horse, the saddle, the lariat, the slicker, and, in popular opinion at least, the Colt six-shooter and the lever-action Winchester rifle. For the gaucho, accoutrements included the horse, the saddle, the lasso, and the poncho, but in addition he used the *boleadoras* (the *bolo*) and the knife, his *facón*. The typical outfit for the cowboy became traditional as did that of the gaucho, which differed markedly from that of the cowboy and showed the influence of the Spanish. The racial origin of most of the gauchos was Spanish; the cowboys were mostly of Western European extraction. The language of the latter was English, sometimes infused with Spanish vocabulary if they had contact with Mexicans. Cowboys drank coffee; gauchos drank *maté*, a tea of *yerba* leaves, sipped through a silver straw from a gourd prepared especially for the purpose. Both cowboys and gauchos rejected menial jobs and preferred the nomadic life of the wanderer, drifting from place to place. They performed the same kind of work with the cattle —branding, castrating, and herding. Cowboys sang as they herded the cattle or as they sat around campfires on drives or in cattle camps. The gauchos did likewise and also frequented the *pulpería*—the equivalent of the saloon— where they sang songs, usually to the accompaniment of a guitar.

From this discussion, one can perceive that although superficial differences in dress and habits did exist, basically the two groups developed in a similar historical-geographical context and both evidence the same traits and general attitudes toward life.

It would be presumptuous to begin a discussion of the entire body of cowboy and gaucho songs or to assume that there is only one perspective evident in these songs. There is, however, a general consistency in the viewpoint, consistent enough at least to offer validity to the generalizations that follow. Without doubt the most complete collection of the songs of the cowboy is found in the various editions of *Cowboy Songs and Other Frontier Ballads* by John Lomax.[3] All of the following excerpts of cowboy songs are from this collection. The 1938 edition, which Lomax did with his son Alan, can be looked upon as the definitive collection of these pieces of folk music. John Lomax collected cowboy songs from his youth in Central Texas along the Chisholm Trail. Encouraged by George Lyman Kittridge and Barrett Wendell at Harvard University, Lomax published the two early editions in 1910 and 1916. His efforts in collecting cowboy songs as well as folk songs of other groups represent a significant accomplishment that led Stith Thompson to call him "Dean of Ballad Hunters."[4] The gauchos had no such singular guardian spirit, but many of the songs are available in Jesús M. Pereyra's *Canto y Guitarra en Cañada de la Cruz*, Alfredo Terrera's *Cantos Tradicionales Argentinos* and *El Caballo Criollo en la tradición Argentina*, Lazaro Flury's *Folklore*, and Marcelino Roman's *Itinerario del Payador*.[5] Obviously the gaucho songs could not be expected to address every topic found in the Lomax canon, and vice versa, but it is easy to demonstrate that as a body, the songs of both groups addressed a general core of common experiences that made cowboy/gaucho life the unique kind of existence that it was.

The land—be it plain or prairie, *llano* or pampa—looms large in the thinking of these outdoorsmen. Both groups express their love of the land in the same romantic, idyllic, and pastoral way. Representative of this category is the song "A Home on the Range," which delineates the cowboy's sentiment for his land:

> Oh, give me a home where the buffalo roam,
> Where the deer and the antelope play,
> Where seldom is heard a discouraging word
> And the skies are not cloudy all day.
>
> (p.425, ll. 1-4)

Undoubtedly, the depiction of the land in this and succeeding stanzas of the song represents a romanticized view of the land. With similar intention, the gaucho, in the next eight-line song, compares the happiness of the linnet in the desert with the awakening of the dawn on the deserted Pampa:

> Y cual jilguero en el monte,
> Que canta de rama en rama
> Y en el desierto derrama
> Las delicias de su canto
> Se oye verter como llanto,
> Y como un eco que implora,
> Cuando la naciente aurora
> Va descubriendo su manto.
>
> (*Folklore*, p.15, ll. 1-8)

[Like the happy linnet, which singing from branch to branch expresses the delight of its song in the desert, a distant voice like a supplicant echo, is heard when the rising dawn with its magnificence, discovers little by little the beauty of the place—the deserted plain.]

The beauty of the broad, flat, treeless plain would definitely be in the eye of the beholder. But to cowboy and gaucho, there is no doubt about the magnificence of their beloved prairies.

Those familiar with Lomax's collection, however, will recall a song entitled "Hell in Texas," a humorous treatment of the harsh nature of the brushy southern and western ranchland in the state, an area preferred by Satan because it has "all that is needed/To make a good hell" (p.318, ll. 23-24). The criticism does seem in jest, a trait of one who loves his land but loves to tell of its harshness.

The kind of work the cowboy did on this land is described in a number of songs. A representative one is "The Black Tail Range":

> I am a roving cowboy off from the Western plains,
> My trade is cinching saddles and pulling bridle reins.
> I can throw a lasso with the most graceful ease,
> And I can rope a bronco and ride him where I please.
>
> (p.293, ll. 1-4)

The cowboy not only is expressing pride in his ability to lasso broncos but also is bragging about his other working skills. Similar is the comment found in stanza III of "The Texas Cowboys":

> But springtime comes at last and finds them glad and gay,
> They ride out on the round-up about the first of May;

About the first of August they start up the trail,
They have to stay with the cattle then no matter rain or hail.

(p.291, ll. 9-12)

Another comment worth citing is found in "The Cowboy at Work":

When the storm breaks in its fury and the lightning's vivid flash
Makes you thank the Lord for shelter and for bed,
Then it is he mounts his pony and away you see him dash,
No protection but the hat upon his head.

(p.83, ll. 9-12)

Additional comment is found in such familiar favorites as "The Old Chisholm Trail" and "Little Joe, the Wrangler" (pp.28-37, 91-93).

Like the cowboy, the gaucho also delights in the art of lassoing and shows his feelings for it in "Creo Pialar y Enlazar":

Creo pialar de payanca;
Codo vuelto, sobre el lomo,
Se enlazar de qualquier modo
Y en cualquier forma que sea
Nunca un gaucho se marea
De pialar una potranca.

(*El Caballo Criollo*, p.167, ll. 1-6)

[I know how to rope broncos; to cast the lasso about their legs, over their back; I know how to lasso in any way I want, because a gaucho never gets dizzy while lassoing a young mare.]

The following song, an untitled one of ten-line stanzas, sketches different moments of the gaucho's work herding cattle and highlights such personal qualities as responsibility, endurance, and dedication. Noticeable first is the gaucho's attitude toward his work:

El por ninguna razón
Abandona su tarea,
Haya sol o truene o llueva
No deja sus animales,
Y derecho a los corrales
Con paciencia los arrea.

(*Canto y Guitarra*, p. 54, ll. 5-10)

[The herder never abandons his work. In sunshine or thunder or rain, he never leaves his animals, and with patience he drives them to the corral.]

Furthermore, he says that neither the hot summer sun nor the work tires him and his horse as they work the entire day. The next stanza refers to the end of the job, when, once he has already gathered the required number of cattle, he starts his ride back to town. "Despacito y con cuidado,/ Siempre arreando su ganado" (ll. 34-35). [Slowly and very carefully he is always driving his cattle.] The speaker affirms that in order not to lose the cattle, the herder's precaution increases in case of unexpected vicissitudes while on the go. Lines 38 to 40 mention that after those rainy nights, the herder always wakes up wet. After depicting such hard moments, the song concludes by warning city people, who generally never consider the herder's work, that the cowman's life is difficult and dangerous.

Likewise, the next song, in a narrative style, stresses the harshness of the gaucho's experience as a herder. The first stanza is the speaker's description of the gaucho driving the animals to the headquarters after he has rounded them up. With explicit images the herder is pictured on a "día de sol ardiente" (l. 2) [hot sunny day], almost unseen because of a thick, dusty cloud:

> Medio ahogado por la tierra
> Viene ciego y jadeante
> Confundidos, resonantes
> Sus silbidos y voceadas,
> Echándose por delante
> Los novillos a pechadas.
> (*Canto y Guitarra*, p.56, ll. 5-10)

[Riding through the heat, almost drowned and blinded for the dust, he drives his cattle, pushing them forward with his whistling and his yelling.]

On the whole, the songs exhibit a gusto for the life and work of cowboys and gauchos. Both kinds of prairie men are romantic, passionate, and eager for life, and they disdain the heat, dust, and danger. The narrator of "Soy Hijo de este Suelo" suggests his attitude toward life:

> Soy el hijo de este suelo
> Soy el alegre paisano
> Soy el gaucho campechano
> . . . .
> Que vive feliz en su rancho
> Hecho de paja y terrón.
> (*Cantos*, p.167, ll. 3-5, 9-10)

[I am the son of this land, the joyful countryman; I am the frank open gaucho, who, happily, lives in his *rancho* made of straw and clay.]

Characteristic comment on this thought is made by the singer in "Doney Gal":

> We whoop at the sun and yell through the hail,
> But we drive the poor dogies on down the trail,
> And we'll laugh at the storms, the sleet and snow,
> When we reach the little town of San Antonio.
>
> (p.10, ll. 15-18)

Indeed, courage and endurance are the traits of the cowman, who challenges nature to perform the chores of his trade. It matters little about the result of the men's enterprise on the trail or at the ranch, because they have to do their work even if it means risking their lives. It often did, and death was a frequent occurrence in this dangerous life.[6] Such a tragedy is recalled by the next stanza in which we learn that a gaucho named Cirilo, while trying to ride an outlaw horse, meets a tragic end:

> Cuando mas confiado estaba,
> El "colorado" se boleaba
> Arrojandolo a la muerte.
>
> (*Canto y Guitarra*, p.52, ll. 42-44)

[Although Cirilo was confident of his abilities, the "red horse" bucked furiously, throwing Cirilo to his death.]

At the same time, both cowboy and gaucho strove to be good friends, honest with their fellow men. "The Melancholy Cowboy" is a good example of this trait, for the man asserts:

> You can go to a cowboy hungry, go to him wet or dry,
> And ask him for a few dollars in change and he will not deny;
>
> (p.220, ll. 9-10)

The frank, candid spirit can also be seen in the gaucho when he expresses that

> Así llega a los rodeos,
> Contento y muy divertido
> Con otros de su partido.
>
> (*Canto y Guitarra*, p.54, ll. 21-23)

[He rides out to the roundup and finds himself and other of his fellow men glad and delighted.]

Cowboys in the 1890s

The men communicate with their fellow cowmen in good terms, but cowboy
and gaucho also interact with God and acknowledge Him as the Father and
Creator. Illustrative is the invocation in the song "The Cowman's Prayer":

> Now, O Lord, please lend me thine ear,
> The prayer of a cattleman to hear;
> No doubt the prayer may seem strange,
> But I want you to bless our cattle range.
>
> (p.330, ll. 1-4)

The religious spirit of the gaucho is seen when—after deprived of God's
help—he asks forgiveness:

> Dios grande y celestial,
> Perdoname si mentí;
> También me diste a mi
> Un don grande y sin igual,
> Puesto que siendo mi mal
> Desengaños y tormentos
> El inmenso sufrimiento
> Que el corazón me desgarra,
> Dios, me diste la guitarra
> Para cantar mi lamento.
>
> (*Canto y Guitarra*, p.30, ll. 31-40)

[Oh Lord, great and celestial, forgive me because I told you a lie; You have
also given me a great gift beyond comparison. Since disillusion and affliction
are my complaints of all my sufferings which tug my heart, oh Lord, You gave
me the guitar to sing my lament.]

Both the cowboy and the gaucho agree in their positive attitudes toward
work and emphasize the endurance and sense of responsibility of the men
while caring for the cattle. Similarly, both sing of their loneliness. The cowboy
comments upon the solitude on the trail and speaks of the trials of his
dangerous and demanding life. Truthful revelations on this peculiarity of
life are the statements of the two following stanzas from the songs "Doney
Gal" and "Diamond Joe," respectively:[7]

> We're alone, Doney Gal, in the rain and hail,
> Got to drive these dogies down the trail:
> Get along, little dogie, on your way.
>
> (p.11, ll. 31-33)

> I am a pore cowboy, I've got no home;
> I'm here today and tomorrow I'm gone;
> I've got no folks, I'm forced to roam;
> Where I hang my hat is home sweet home.
>   (pp.65-66, ll. 5-8)

On the other hand, the gaucho forgets himself, magnifying instead the horse as a central part of all his life—remembering his happy days with his horse or lamenting his old age and the impossibility of riding the animal again. Representative is this passage from "Mi Tropilla," in which he remembers his horses and says:

> Hoy estoy viejo y de a pie
> Y vivo rememorando,
> Y he de morir añorando
> Los pingos que yo ensillé.
>   (*El Caballo Criollo*, p.189, ll. 1-4)

[I am old and without my horse; but I will live remembering and grieving, until I die, for the horses that I saddled.]

"Mi Tropilla," a ten-line stanza poem with a quatrain as an introduction, relates the gaucho's recollection of all the good times he remembers from his youth. Hence, in the first stanza the old gaucho comments that he would like to reveal which of all his horses were the best, but there were so many in his life that he cannot even remember them. Therefore, in search of an easy way of recalling, the man analyzes the different opportunities for which he needed a horse, such as to go to work, to go horseback riding with his girlfriend, or to go to school as a child. Among the different horses in the gaucho's life, he recalls:

> Se llamba "Coquetón"
> Sangre de toro, lindon,
> Goloso pa' galopiar.
>   (*El Caballo Criollo*, p.189, ll. 20-22)

[His name was *Coquetón*, a full blooded and beautiful horse eager to gallop.]

With *Coquetón* (a male flirt), the gaucho rode to town to court the girls. After *Coquetón* he remembers *Corazón* (heart):

> Cuando había que carnear,
> Era pingo de enlazar

> Dejarlo tirando el lazo
> Siguro a desjarratear
>   (p.190, ll. 30-34)

[Exceptional in the work, it was an animal good for lassoing and slaughtering cattle.]

Stanza V, more than a reminiscence of old times, is the gaucho's appreciation of horses in general. He says that a good horse is seen everywhere—in a rodeo, in the roundup, on the trails, in town carrying a lady, in a tournament jumping, or on the plain running behind an ostrich, the South American rhea.

Finally, after pointing out the multiple talents of the horse, the old gaucho concludes his song:

> Sin ninguna distinción
> Pa' mi fueron puntos altos
> Sobre ese velo va un manto
> Con la siguiente inscripción
> Que llevo en mi corazón
> Al Pichón y al Suerte al Salto.
>   (p.190, ll. 49-54)

[Without any distinction all the horses were the best. But I still remember in my heart *Pichón* and *Suerte al Salto*.]

Although *Pichón* and *Suerte al Salto* stood out in the old gaucho's mind, as the song suggests, the gaucho remembers all the horses in a favorable way.

The cowboy and the gaucho, equally in love with their horses, share the same idea that a cattleman without a horse is nothing. Characteristic is this expression of the Spanish poet: "Cómo me siento más hombre/Cuando me veo a caballo! [How much of a man I feel when I see myself on a horse!] The cowboys loved and respected their horses, even the ones that were outlaws, as seen in "The Skew-Ball Black" (pp.14-15). In it, a young would-be cowboy is bucked off, barely escaping serious injury in the incident, and is ridiculed by the veterans gathered to watch the show. In "Pinto," the cowboy laments that a famous bucking horse dies before he has a chance to ride it (pp.73-74). One song in the cowboy's repertoire not related to cowboy life is "Bonnie Black Bess," obviously of English origin but nonetheless appealing to the western American herdsmen because of the faithfulness and spirit of the black mare which allows her highwayman rider to elude pursuit. When threatened with capture, he kills her "through kindness" to keep her from falling into the hands of his enemies (pp.217-20). Jack Thorp, the earliest collector of cowboy songs, wrote one called "Speckles" that Lomax included as "Chopo" in his early edition of *Cowboy Songs and Other Frontier Ballads*. It is certainly a complimentary song concerning the value of a horse with spirit although not necessarily with beauty:

> You're a good roping horse, you were never jerked down,
> When tied to a steer, you will circle him round;
> Let him once cross the string and over he'll go,—
> You sabe the business, my cow-horse, Chopo.
>
> (p.371, ll. 13-16)

One of the most famous songs is "The White Steed of the Prairies," certainly a laudatory song for the beautiful white stallion that defies capture. The last stanza waxes artificially eloquent on the famous animal:

> His fields have no fence save the mountain and sky;
> His drink the snow-capped Cordilleras supply;
> 'Mid the grandeur of nature sole monarch is he,
> His gallant heart swells with the pride of the free.
>
> (p.228, ll. 29-32)

Cowboys may have loved horses more than women, and they may have had more success with the animals than with the opposite sex. In love, cowboys and gauchos are rarely successful, according to the songs. The men face the same unfaithfulness and forgetfulness from the women they love. Both lament the girl who has abandoned the roamer for another lover closer to home or who has not returned love. The song "The Lovesick Cowboy" comments on this particularly sad relationship:

> I am a bold cowboy, from Midland I came,
> But my virtue's departed, I'm covered with shame;
> The cold darts of Cupid have wrought me much grief,
> My heart's burst asunder, I can find no relief.
>
> (p.268, ll. 1-4)

Another young cowboy leaves the daughter of a nearby rancher to "cross the plains." She promises to wait for his return, but after he has left Texas and arrived in Tombstone, Arizona, he receives a letter telling him that she has married another man. His spirit broken, the young man refuses to work and turns to gambling. The song "The Rambling Cowboy" closes on this note of warning:

Come all you reckless and rambling boys who have listened to this song,
If it hasn't done you any good, it hasn't done you any wrong;
But when you court a pretty girl, just marry her while you can,
For if you go across the plains she'll marry another man.

(p.194, ll. 21-24)

Certainly, the man is not at his best when he feels frustrated in love with an unfaithful girl. As in the above song, the gaucho bemoans his misfortune in love in this stanza:

Llora la torcacita
Con triste gemir,
Yo lloro con ella
Por el bien que perdí.
(*Folklore*, p.27, ll. 1-4)

[The little ring-dove cries with sad moan; and I, like her, cry for the love I have lost.]

In a broader sense, when the subject matter of the songs is related to women in general, men agree that it is wise to be cautious in dealing with the fairer sex, because women usually prove to be untrue anyway. Such is the assertion of the cowboy, who says, "Don't depend on a woman—you're beat if you do" (*"The Lovesick Cowboy,"* p.269, l. 18). Similarly, the gaucho sings:

Las mujeres son zainas
Y otras overas,
Son muy sonsos los hombres
Que fían de las polleras.
(*Cantos*, p.217, ll. 5-8)

[Some women are like mischievous horses, and others are like speckled ones; silly are men who trust these women.]

In general, cowboys and gauchos are opposed to matrimony or long relationships with women because such arrangements deprive men of the freedom essential to their way of life. Representative is this stanza from "The Range Riders":

But when you get married, boys, you are done with this life,
You have sold your sweet comfort for to gain you a wife;
Your wife she will scold you, and the children will cry.

(p.280, ll. 13-15)

Understandably, the gaucho prefers his freedom and his horse to being united with his lady forever. An example is the following statement:

> Mi caballo y mi mujer
> Se me fueron para Salta,
> Que vuelva mi caballito
> Mi mujer no me hace falta.
>
> (*Cantos*, p.224, ll. 1-4)

[My horse and my lady went to Salta; I want only my little horse to return because I do not need my lady.]

The cowboy songs tend to be more casual than philosophical except in some of the pieces related to religious themes. The gaucho songs contain both casual and philosophical elements, but the majority of these songs have deep metaphysical meanings, characteristic of a reflective, meditative attitude toward life. The cowboy might drink wildly, as the song "Rye Whisky" suggests (pp.163-66), and he might brag outrageously, as in "The Boasting Drunk in Dodge" (pp.135-36). But he could also, as in "Silver Jack," impose his mother's religion, by force if necessary, on an unbeliever. As Jack explains the Christian precepts to his antagonist in the ballad, the man accepts the faith, even acknowledging the divinity of Christ under Jack's "bare knuckle" evangelism (pp.234-36). "The long, low whistle" of the cowboy and " lo mejor de sue cantar" [the best of his singing] of the gaucho remind us that despite being separated by vast distances, the two cultures developed remarkable similarities in methods of handling cattle as well as in attitudes toward their work and life in general. The loneliness and danger of the work are shared experiences, experiences reflected in the songs that have survived from the day when the old-time cowboy and gaucho led free, open lives.

Notes

1. For a treatment of the history of the development of the range cattle industry and the gaucho in Argentina, see Ricardo Rojas, *Historia de la Literature Argentina*, Vol. I, *Los Gauchescos* (Buenos Aires: Editorial Losada A.A., 1948); Pedro Paoli, *Trayectoria del Gaucho* (Sante Fe: Universidad Nacional del Litoral, 1948); and Arturo Scarone, *El Gaucho* (Montevideo: Maximo Garcia Monografía Sintética Historico-Literaria, 1922). In English see Madaline W. Nichols, *The Gaucho, Cattle Hunter, Cavalryman, Ideal of Romance* (Durham, N.C.: Duke University Press, 1942); and Edward Tinker, *The Horsemen of the Americas and the Literature They Inspired* (Austin: University of Texas Press, 1967).

2. See Walker D. Wyman, *The Wild Horse of the West* (Lincoln: University of Nebraska Press, 1945); and J. Frank Dobie, *The Longhorns* (Boston: Little, Brown and Company, 1941).

3. John A. Lomax and Alan Lomax, *Cowboy Songs and Other Frontier Ballads*, 3rd ed. (New York: Macmillan, 1938). Two earlier editions were done without the assistance of Alan. One was issued in 1910 by Sturgis and Walton Co., New York; the second with forty additional songs was issued in 1916 by the same publisher. (Citations in the text are from the 1938 edition unless indicated otherwise.)

4. Stith Thompson, "John Avery Lomax (1867–1948)," *Journal of American Folklore* 61 (July 1948): 305.

5. Jesús M. Pereyra, *Canto y Guitarra en Cañada de la Cruz* (La Plata: Ministerio de Educación Subsecrataria de Cultura, 1970); Alfredo Terrera, *Cantos Tradicionales Argentinos* (Buenos Aires: A. Peña Lillo-Editor, 1967); Terrera, *El Caballo Criollo en la tradición Argentina* (Buenos Aires: Editorial Patria Vieja, 1970); Lazaro Flury, *Folklore* (Puebla, Mexico: Editorial Jose M. Cajica, Jr., Sx. A., 1973); Marcelino Roman, *Itinerario del Payador* (Buenos Aires: Editorial Lautaro, 1957).

6. Well-known songs about death include "Little Joe, the Wrangler," "Utah Carrol," "Charlie Rutledge," and others.

7. For a discussion of the portrayal of life in the songs, see Lawrence Clayton, "Elements of Realism in the Songs of the Cowboy," in Christopher S. Durer et al., eds., *Proceedings of the Second University of Wyoming American Studies Conference: American Renaissance and American West* (Laramie: University of Wyoming Press, 1981), pp. 31-39.

8 For a discussion of the debate between Thorp and Lomax over this song and others, see John O. West, "Jack Thorp and John Lomax: Oral or Written Transmission?" *Western Folklore* 26 (April 1967): 113-18.

Heaven

by James Ward Lee

Among the ancients much more was written about Hell than about Heaven. Among the Greeks, the Hebrews, and the Norse—those whose writings we study most in the Western World—Heaven was a place where the gods dwelled. No mortals were admitted—at least not early in the mythologies of those peoples. Things were simple and clear: the gods lived in Heaven; living mortals, on earth; the dead, in Hell. It was fairly late in the various traditions that a place for humans was found in the land of the immortals. Late in Greek history a place was found for heroes that corresponded to Heaven, and famous Greek warriors were transported to the Isles of the Blest—often called the Elysian Fields or Happy Isles. Similarly, Valhalla was invented as a place for the Norse heroes. And, finally, we learn in the Old Testament that a few pious Hebrews were admitted into the presence of God—Elisha, Lazarus, and a scant few others.

It was not until the death and resurrection of Jesus Christ that man was accorded much space in what Mark Twain's Emmaline Grangerford calls "the realms of the Good and the Great." The mass of Hebrews—like most Greeks and Norsemen—went to a pale, dark world of shadows either to languish forever or to suffer the tortures of the damned. Those who had sinned in a particular way were given a punishment suitable to the sin. Among the Greeks, each punishment was unique; for instance, Tantalus was the only one placed nipple-deep in cool, clear water with an ever-retreating apple tree just outside his grasp. Then there was Sisyphus and his rock. The Jews and Christians went in for group punishment—generic punishment—with all adulterers in one place and all murderers in another. Of course most of the

65

inhabitants in Hell went unpunished, if we can consider that living for eternity in a world of half-light is not punishment. Dante tells us that the virtuous pagans who were consigned to Hell were being punished by being denied the sight of God.

Early in the Christian era, the picture of Heaven changed. Christ released many from the netherworld when he harrowed Hell, but about all we know of their change of venue is that they were freed from Hell to live with God and the angels forever and forever. Likewise, the picture of Hell changed, and from the days of the Church Fathers to the time of Milton, the Christian world received increasingly distinct descriptions of Hades. We went from generalized fire, brimstone, and gnashing of teeth to the carefully and meticulously described Nine Circles of Dante's *Inferno*, to the Lake of Brimstone that Satan finds himself and his minions on in Book One of *Paradise Lost*. Dante paints the best pictures of Hell, but Milton is not far behind. Both were as mean as a pair of junkyard Dobermans, and both were anxious to create fitting places for their enemies. The result is a geography of Hell that has kept Christian children in nightmares for centuries and has informed the sermons of revival preachers since the time of the Great Awakening and of radio and television evangelists since the time of Signor Marconi. Dante and Milton and their followers could make Hell sound as mean as Houston's Second Ward on a Friday night. But despite their interest in the afterlife, Dante and Milton were washouts when it came to describing Heaven. Neither one could think of anything more delicious than blinding light and streets paved with gold. They and their preacher friends in Puritan pulpits made Hell sound like Teheran under the Ayatollah, but Heaven was as bland as one of the scenes from *The Sound of Music*.

In Heaven, one walks on golden streets, is enclosed by a jasper wall, and can see mortal life down below by looking out from the Pearly Gates. The food is milk and honey—one clogs the arteries and the other causes sugar diabetes. The folklore about Heaven that has crept into our tradition may be partly the result of the dreams of discontented Middle Easterners who lived off boiled sheep meat, slept to the mournful brays of lovesick camels, and spent days and nights living in tents made from odiferous animal hides. After such an earthly existence, almost any kind of vaguely described afterlife seems heavenly.

Even in the enlightened nineteenth century, an era of intense questioning, Heaven was not much speculated upon. We were almost a third of the way into the twentieth century before mortals got down to cases about the landscape of Heaven. For a good part of our century, Heaven was simply "The land beyond the river / That they call the Great Forever. " If it got described at all, it was in the most general of terms. One stood on

> Jordan's stormy banks . . .
> And cast a wistful eye
> To Caanan's fair and happy land.

Over there on the other side of "the Jordan," one could hear the angels singing; one could rest on that beautiful shore.

The quotations above are from gospel songs. Gospel songwriters—modern musical popularizers of religious themes and explicators of theological matters—are responsible for resurrecting Heaven from the neglect of the ages. The authors of our favorite gospel songs began slowly to depict the kind of life that we can expect in "the Sweet By and By." Early in the "heavenly era" of the modern gospel song, we get the following description of Heaven from the Reverend A. S. Bridgewater and Mr. A. P. Bland:

> In Heaven no drooping nor pining.
> No wishing for elsewhere to be.
> God's light is forever there shining,
> How beautiful Heaven must be.
>
> Pure waters of life there are flowing,
> And all who will drink may be free.
> Rare Jewels of Splendor are glowing,
> How beautiful Heaven must be.

Heaven in "How Beautiful Heaven Must Be" is not particularized; in fact, the song does not go much beyond Dante's idea of Heaven as a place of shining and glowing.

We get more in Arthur T. Ingler's 1929 song about life in Glory.

> There's a holy and beautiful city
> Whose builder and ruler is God.
> John saw it descending from Heaven
> When Patmos, in exile, he trod.
>
> Its high massive wall is of Jasper,
> The city itself is pure gold,
> And when my frail tent here is folded,
> Mine eyes shall its glory behold.

> In that bright city, pearly white city
> I have a mansion, an harp and a crown.

The song that O. A. Parris wrote in 1944 was a bit more modest in its desire than the one Ingler had written fifteen years before. Parris merely wanted "a cabin in the corner of gloryland" where he could "hear the angels sing and shake Jesus' hand." Mr. Parris apparently did not feel as worthy as Mr. Ingler did—or perhaps it was a matter of zoning in Heaven. Real estate motifs do begin to show up in the Heaven of the gospel songs. The first that I know of appears in J. C. Leroy's song "When I Can Read My Title Clear," words that Leroy set to an Isaac Watts tune.

> When I can read my title clear,
> To Mansions in the skies,
> And bid farewell to every fear
> And wipe my weeping eyes.

Leroy must be a real estate developer: note the plural "mansions." Not just one little cabin for old J. C.

In Roark Bradford's *Old Man Adam and His Chillen*, which was adapted for the stage as *Green Pastures*, we can see many of the folk roots that helped create the Heaven of the spirituals—black and white—and the gospel songs. In the stories by Bradford and the play by Marc Connally, the reader/audience is given the black people's folk heaven. But it doesn't differ much from the view we get of the Celestial Realm in the white gospel songs. At the opening of the play, we are treated to a fish fry in Heaven where the "biled custard" is a little thin because of the lack of "firmament." God is asked by one of the good sisters to create some more. God overdoes it and has to create some place to "dreen off the firmament." So, more or less by accident, the Lawd creates the earth and all that therein is. He laments the problems caused by passing a miracle and says, "That the trouble when you pass a miracle; you just has to rare back and pass another one." See how beautiful Heaven must be! And how human!

Old Man Adam and His Chillen came out in 1928 and *Green Pastures* in 1930. The same years mark the beginning of the heyday of the gospel songs about Heaven. It is true that Heaven played a large part in the black and white spirituals of the nineteenth century, but those songs did not get down to the details, descriptions, and designs like the gospel songs of this century did—and do.

Not only do the songs about Heaven describe all the landscapes one might see in Heaven, they also tell a great deal about the population of the "pearly white city." Who will be waiting on the other side of "Jordan's stormy banks" to greet us? Nearly everybody we have ever heard of! The rules for admission have been relaxed greatly since the days of Dante and Milton. Back then, hardly anybody but close friends of the poets and major-league saints had a ghost of a chance of getting in. In fact, in the Heavens of Dante and Milton, a lot of the finest saints failed to make the cut. Nowadays, the rules for getting in are about as tough as for getting in to one of Jay Gatsby's parties—and not nearly as stringent as the standards for admission to popular New York nightspots. My cousin J. T. had a garish, rubberized spare-tire cover on his Model-A Ford that said, "Go ahead and pass, Hell ain't but half full." This forerunner of the bumpersticker was right. Nobody has gone to Hell in years if you can believe the hillbilly songs and the gospel songs and the positive-thinking TV preachers. (And if you can't believe Roy Acuff and Norman Vincent Peale, who can you believe?) In fact, the last known inhabitant of Hell was Don Juan in Shaw's play—and he went because he wanted to, because he found Heaven too boring. But then he hadn't heard all about the "new" Heaven.

The twentieth-century Heaven of story, song, play, and sermon will be full. All Hillbilly singers who were killed outright in car wrecks and plane crashes get to go, as well as those who became sick and died from TB, alcoholism, drug abuse, venereal diseases, and sugar diabetes. Hillbilly Heaven, as Tex Ritter sang about it before he died and went there, has Patsy Cline, Jim Reeves, Jimmy Rogers, Cowboy Copas, Lefty Frizell, Moon Mullican, Hank Williams, Bob Wills (and assorted Texas Playboys), and Ernest Tubb. And places are being reserved for Willie and Waylon and the Boys; for Eddie Arnold, Loretta Lynn, and Dolly Parton; for Tammy and George and their various wives and husbands. ("We're not the jet set; we're the old Chevrolett set; we're the Jones and Wynette set, but ain't we got love.") In fact, there is going to be a whole part of Heaven that will sound a lot like Opryland, U.S.A.

And don't forget the Righteous Brothers' "Rock 'n Roll Heaven." One of the brighter stars in that pantheon is Buddy Holly—that goes without saying since he died young. And in a plane wreck. And in the same fiery crash as Richie Havens and the Big Bopper, who, needless to say, joined Holly— all singing "Chantilly Lace." Merle Haggard has just added "the King," the late Elvis, who did not die because of TB, sugar diabetes, a flood, a famine, a gunshot, or a plane crash. In fact, if the *Midnight Globe* is to be believed, he may not be dead at all but may be down in Florida being kept alive on tubes along with the Kennedys, J. Edgar Hoover, Hitler, and Dr. Mengele. But if he is indeed dead, then there is no question about his induction into the "Bop, Bop, a Loo Bop Hall of Fame."

Heaven will not, of course, be occupied solely by saints and by singers of hillbilly and rock songs. The military and the political world will be well represented. Those who remember World War II will remember "There's a Star-Spangled Banner Waving Somewhere," written to honor the memory of Colin P. Kelly, Jr., who heroically flew his fighter plane down the smokestack of the *Haruna Maru*. (It wasn't called *Kamikaze* when one of us did it in 1942.) In that song, we get a catalog of war heroes. The narrator is a little crippled boy who can't serve his country; he sings:

> There's a star-spangled banner waving somewhere
> In a distant land so many miles away.
> Only Uncle Sam's great heroes get to go there
> Where I wish that I could also live some day.
> I'd see Lincoln, Custer, Washington, and Perry
> And Nathan Hale and Colin Kelly too.

It may seem odd that such a controversial figure as George Armstrong Custer should be in Heaven, but, remember, almost everyone gets to go. Anyway, this is not the first sighting of the hero of Little Big Horn. He shows up in Heaven in a song written in 1933—"The Last Round-up."

> I'm headin' for the last round-up;
> There'll be Buffalo Bill with his long snow white hair;
> There'll be Kit Carson and Custer waitin' there
> A-ridin' in the last round-up.
>
> I'm headin' for the last round-up
> To the far away ranch, to the Boss in the sky
> Where the strays are counted and branded, there go I;
> I'm headin' for the last round-up.

We can see, I think, from these songs, both sacred and profane, that most cowboys, wranglers, camp cooks, newsboys, hoboes, railroad men—strays of all sorts that need to be "counted and branded"—will go to join the singers, soldiers, saints, and mothers who will gather "when the roll is called up yonder." Some will go by train, some by plane, some by ship, and some by wading across to the "land beyond the river that they call the great forever."

Daddy Caxton, in A. P. Carter's famous song, will, "when his earthly race is over and the curtains round him fall," be carried "home to victory on the Wabash Cannon Ball." Amelia Earhart, if Dave McEnery's song is true, will make a perfect three-point landing in Beulah Land.

> There's a beautiful, beautiful field
> Far away in a land that is fair.
> Happy landings to you, Amelia Earhart,
> Farewell, first lady of the air.

But millions will go by ship:

> The old ship of Zion, still sailing today
> And gathering her pilgrims along on life's way.
> She's landing her millions, and still landing more,
> The saved of all ages on some fairer shore.

If the Ship of Zion—one of the earliest of the "love boats for Jesus"—is booked, all one has to do is call the other shipping line in order to "Make a trip on the good old Gospel ship/And go sailing through the air. " If making a reservation on either of these ships is a problem, there is a number to call. Just punch a few buttons and

> Telephone to Glory, O what a joy divine,
> I can feel the current moving on the line.
> Built by God the Father, for his loved and own,
> We may talk to Jesus, thru this royal telephone.

"The Royal Telephone," by F. M. Lehman, proves that God the Father antedates Ma Bell in suggesting that we "reach out and touch someone."

Besides all the people who are transported to Heaven by various conveyances, there are the animals—the bovine strays mentioned in "The Last Round-up," not to mention Old Shep and his canine brethren and sistren.

> Now old Shep has gone where the good doggies go.
> And no more with old Shep will I roam,
> But if dogs have a heaven, there's one thing I know:
> Old Shep has a wonderful home.

And there may even be fleas. After all, David Harum, in Edward Wescott's novel of the same name, says, "a reasonable amount of fleas is good for a dog—they keep him from broodin' on bein' a dog." The fleas certainly fit in with E. M. Forster's scene in *A Passage to India* in which the Hindus confound the missionaries by worrying about whether wasps will be allowed in the Christian Heaven. Well, if the flies and wasps and mosquitoes do get in, Heaven begins to look a lot like Houston, Texas. There will be a theme park like Astroworld, a couple of airports, a railway station, a ship channel, a stockyard (for the strays), mansions and shacks side by side (remember there is no zoning either in Houston or in Heaven), and a stadium where Jesus can drop-kick backsliders through the goalposts of life if He needs to.

But there won't be much backsliding in Heaven. In fact, nothing at all will go wrong on the other side of "Jordan's stormy banks." In a gospel songbook called *Gems of Gladness*, a 1933 song by J. E. Roan, "Death Will Never Knock on Heaven's Door," says, "No more open graves, no sad good-byes/ They'll be gone for evermore." And James C. Moore's 1944 song "Where We'll Never Grow Old" says in the refrain:

> Never grow old, where we'll never grow old,
> In a land where we'll never grow old.
> Never grow old, where we'll never grow old,
> In a land where we'll never grow old.

Amen! Let me repeat that: Amen!

Best of them all, when it comes to getting specific about the eternal bliss that is Heaven, is F.M. Lehman's "No Disappointment in Heaven," published in 1942 by the Nazarene Publishing House (with harmony by Miss Claudia Lehman).

> We'll never pay rent for our mansion,
> Our taxes will never come due,
> Our garments will never grow threadbare,
> But always be fadeless and new.

> There'll never be crape on the
>   doorknobs,
> No funeral train in the sky.
> No graves on the hillside of Glory,
> For there we shall nevermore die.

The only worry of any sort that the songwriters express is the one put most articulately by Johnson Oatman, Jr., and William M. Goldman.

> I have changed with the changing seasons,
> And I am bent with toil and care;
> Do you think she will remember,
> Will my mother know me there.

Bet on it! Lovers, too, will be reunited.

> Someday when we meet up yonder,
> We'll stroll hand in hand again,
> In the land that knows no parting,
> Blue eyes crying in the rain.

Wait. Here is one thought. What is going to happen when all mothers and their various husbands and all the Honky-Tonk Angels (admitted because of their storied hearts of gold) get to Heaven? If all these reunions begin to take place, and everybody knows everybody, and everybody gets to "strolling hand in hand," there may be some blue eyes scratched out "in the land that knows no parting."

But if fights do break out in the "pearly white city" it can't add much to the noise that will be going on already. Add to the Heavenly choirs all the harp twanging and off-key singing of the apprentices—Mark Twain says it will be awful because no one practices here on earth. Think of all the discordant tuning-up of all the hillbilly singers who were killed outright or sickened and died of TB, alcohol, drug abuse, or sugar diabetes. Throw in the performers of Rock 'N Roll Heaven—Buddy Holly cutting down on "Peggy Sue," the Big Bopper with "Chantilly Lace," Bill Hailey firing the Comets up on "Rock Around the Clock," and the late Elvis (who died from neither earthquake, fire, flood, pestilence, nor sugar diabetes) doing "You Ain't Nothing but a Hound Dog"—and it is going to sound like Jerry Lee singing "Great Balls of Fire" while the Mormon Tabernacle Choir intones "How Great Thou Art" in the background.

There is more to add to the racket. Here'll come Daddy Caxton on the Wabash Cannon Ball—just "listen to the jingle, the rumble and the roar"—and Amelia Earhart in her 1937 monoplane with no muffler. The Ship of Zion and the Good Old Gospel Ship both blowing foghorns and whistles as they come down the River Jordan. And don't forget Brevet Major General George Armstrong Custer and his cavalry troop followed by Sitting Bull, Crazy Horse, and about a zillion Dakota Sioux. And babies. Heaven is packed with infants.

> Full blooming flowers alone will not do.
> Some must be young and ungrown,
> So the frail buds he is gathering too.
> Beautiful gems for his throne.

Well, when the racket gets loud and the babies start to squall and the Indians set up a whoop chasing Custer and Kit Carson and Buffalo Bill and all the trains and planes and pedestrians start arriving and the harps and electric guitars and amplified Kretsch drum sets get tuned up and Milton's fallen angels start a counteroffensive and the wives and former wives and ex-wives get to taking on, it is not hard to see why Don Juan (rhymes with true one) took off. He wasn't, as Shaw thought, bored. He was going deaf! It is also easy to see why Milton and Dante avoided greatly detailed descriptions of such a raucous place and focused their descriptive powers instead on the ice, the fire, the "darkness visible," and the relative quiet of Hell. Even the intrepid Willie Nelson of Abbott-near-Waco in Central Texas couldn't bring himself to face up to the problem of describing the afterlife. All he says is

> Heaven ain't walking on a street paved with gold,
> And Hell ain't a mountain of fire;
> Heaven is laying in my sweet baby's arms,
> And Hell is when Baby's not there.
>
> My front tracks are headed for a cold-water well
> And my back tracks are covered with snow;
> Sometimes it's Heaven and sometimes it's Hell,
> And sometimes I don't even know.

The Old-Time Cowboy Inside Out

by Paul Patterson

We learned in El Paso that the old-time cowboy was in no ways wise sex-wise; now, how was he otherwise? Though he projected himself as the realist's realist he was an idealist in the "purest ray serene" (Gray's "Elegy in a Country Churchyard," Stanza 14). That is, he continued to look at life as he thought it ought to be instead of what it was fast becoming. In Larry McMurtry's *In a Narrow Grave* we see his prodigal Uncle John riding away from the Matador's roundup wagon after fall works had finished for the year—and for Uncle John forever. As he reins his old cow pony into a newer way of cowboying, he is at the point of tears. This is the story of almost all old-time cowboys' lives.

All were in perpetual mourning for what used to be and what still ought to be: Ab Blocker mourning the passing of the long, longhorn trails; Bob Beverly mourning the passing of the open range; my brother John mourning the breaking up of big outfits into small ones; and finally myself lamenting the chuck wagon's replacement with a chuck truck which was, in turn, replaced by pick-ups hauling vittles from the house. And, finally, woe is me, seeing Dairy Queens taking over. (As God is my witness, I have witnessed horsemen in spurs and horses in trailers stopping at this fast food establishment in Crane.)

Matter of fact, authentic cowboys in cafes are getting to be a common sight at Crane's old Sirloin House. Case in point: Bod Smith, fourth generation cowman, in the early morning hours of September 29, 1981, assembled seventeen horse-riding cow-working cowboys there for breakfast. In deference to the old days and the old ways, no doubt, they were respectably and respect-

75

fully attired—with weathered and *un*feathered hats and spurs and boots a cowboy's cowboy would not be ashamed to be caught dead in. Contrast this with the sad and sordid spectacle I witnessed with my own tear-filled eyes at a recent cow-works on the noted Booger Y, once the epitome of wild and western traditions. Leading this drive was a helicopter and fanned out across the sandhills was the oddest assortment of cowpersons ever to grace (or rather *dis*grace) a horse. Yes, a most obscene scene to the idealist, the traditionalist, the un-reconstructed romanticist—horsebackers in tennis shoes, in gimme caps, shirtless, and *even in shorts, for God sakes*!

Although this motley crew penned a few cattle, they spilled the bunch they were really after, foremost amongst which was a seven-year-old, 1900-pound wide-horned steer and thirty or forty wild bulls. Borrowing a line from Dickens' Bob Cratchit I shouted, "God Bless you every one," meaning the escapees, of course. Had my eyes not been too blinded with tears I would have joined them—the escapees, of course.

In fairness to posterity and to the helicopter pilot—truly a remarkable cowboy—and to the Boyd boys now running the Booger Y, plus the three or four other authentic cowboys present, the escapees would have escaped the wildest, wisest old-time cowboy who ever forked a horse. (The pilot told me that these current Booger Y cattle, and another bunch in Hudspeth County, were the wildest in Texas.) It sorrows me to say so, but even some of the authentic cowboys present were not clad in strict accordance with the old-time cowboy's dress code.

The night I graduated from Rankin High School in 1929 I gathered my three graduation gifts and took up bachelor's quarters on a ranch at the foot of King Mountain in Upton County. Among these graduation gifts was a pair of house shoes, comfortable to the Nth degree compared to boots. Yet to have worn them, even in the privacy of my lonely quarters, would have been a gross insult to the noble calling. Consequently, house work as well as horse work was carried on in boots—high-heeled ones in those days. The sensible heel was yet to be introduced. I also kept my spurs on, for practical as well as traditional reasons. It was one way of warding off that vast and lonely silence that encompasses one roundabout when totally alone. Besides, I liked the ring and sing of them, the music therefrom as soothing to soul and spirit as that from today's cowboy's tape deck or stereo.

May I digress here to say that some old-time cowboys—Buck Harmon for one—stayed six months in a line camp without seeing a single human soul. My longest stretch alone was nine days. Even then I took to talking to my two tomcats. Nothing particularly unusual about that—except that my two tomcats took to talking back to me!

On top of this I kept my hat on at all times, except for sleeping. Joe Bailey Rogers, my boss, experienced a hat incident that illustrates my point. A year or so after his marriage he and Edith were aroused in the dead hours of the night by smoke and crackling flames. With the house already half consumed by fire it allowed each only time enough to snatch his or her most prized possession. Joe Bailey escaped with his hat and Edith with the baby.

For an unreconstructed traditionalist like myself the unkindest cut of all is the sad state into which cowboy clothes have sunk. They have been bought up and bastardized by "cowboys" the world around—from Timbuctoo to Kalamazoo, from rockbound coasts of Maine to the sunny slopes of Spain. Specifically, your midnight cowboy, your rhinestone cowboy, your cocaine cowboy, your urban cowboy, and your asphalt cowboy. (Now your asphalt cowboy is not to be confused with your "ass-fault" cowboy. Your asphalt cowboy is the one jockeying the eighteen-wheelers up and down the asphalt; whereas your ass-fault cowboy is the one making an ass of himself on his CB radio, and it's nobody's fault but his own.)

Can't say as I blame these phonies for dressing thus—like us. The gods of fashion must be appeased. Besides, some of these dudes do look sharp, not to mention *muy mucho macho*, as they say in El Paso. That is to say, of all of these hordes of ersatz cowboys there is only one I would like to introduce to old Flaxey, the horse that caused this left collarbone to stand out half an inch farther than the other one. Last fall this "cowboy" appeared in the first of a series on American Culture—manners, mores, morals, etc. Guess what state was featured first. Texas, of course, Houston, Texas, of which state and city this "cowboy" was king, alone and on his own, filling our middle-class, twenty-one-inch TV screen. To paraphrase "Streets of Laredo," "I could see by his outfit that he was a cowboy" etc. By *outfit* I speak in reference to hat only which was all I saw or cared to see. As regards the audio, one strident utterance was all I heard or cared to hear, the utterance being one obscene, four-letter word, a far cry from the old-time cowboy's cowboy who would not utter such a word in the presence of *one* female let alone several million. This is the only type of cowboy I would forbid the wearing of cowboy clothes or a facsimile thereof.

September of 1930 I enrolled in the University at Austin but dared not wear my first pair of genuine shop-made cowboy boots lest I be taken for the hick that I was. Last fall I appeared on that same campus to tell cowboy tales but dared not wear my current cowboy boots lest I come face to face with that Houston "cowboy," the other end of whose outfit might turn out to be boots identical to mine.

Now then, as regards your old-time cowboy's regard for others; by others I mean those other than cowboys. Generous to a fault but with other faults as well, foremost among which was a degree of intolerance for those whose heritage, background, life styles, music appreciation, race, religion, language, sense of humor, politics, etc. differed from his own. That is to say, he was a redneck from head to heel.

Here's what I mean: A friend of mine from Fredericksburg tells of his father who, as a young man, drifted out around Midland to try his hand at cowboying on a wider, wilder scale. Shortly, however, he returned home disillusioned, despondent, discouraged. Not that he was not strong, courageous, skillful, and willing. It was just that a man "ought not to speak the English language so damned peculiar. Or wear a hat at such a gawdalmighty angle—a squattin' on his head like a bullfrog fixin' to hop." Or, say, like taking offense at being dipped for ticks even after he had just crossed into a quarantined area.

Even though relegated to the wagon tongue at meal time (the cowboy's equivalent of the Jim Crow section) the black cowboy fared better than the Mexican or German or other immigrant counterpart. After all, the black cowboy ate the same grub and spoke the same language (after a fashion) that the whites did. Besides, the black cowboy was the white one's equal—many times superior—in any horseback game you could name. So was the Mexican, but like the new immigrant, he talked so damned funny, ate such peculiar grub, and worshipped God in such unGodly ways; hence was not to be trusted.

Larry McMurtry (*In a Narrow Grave*) goes even farther by including the farmer: "A one-gallus farmer ranked very low in their esteem, and there were McMurtrys who would champion the company of Negroes and Mexicans over the company of farmers—particularly if the farmers happened to be Germans. The land just to the north of the McMurtry holdings was settled by an industrious colony of German dairymen, and the Dutchmen (as they were called) were thought to be a ridiculous and unsightly thorn in the fair flesh of the range."

McMurtry goes on to say, "The cowboy's contempt of the farmer was not unmixed with pity. The farmer walked in the dust all his life, a hard and ignominious fate." Yet farmers should not feel put down by this. Cowboys felt this way about kings and princes, potentates and presidents, generals and tycoons, an attitude made possible by the horse upon whose back sat a saddle which was the throne upon which and from which the king cowboy surveyed all that he possessed—which was the universe!

I heard an old-time cowboy's testimonial at Bloys Cowboy Camp Meeting in the Davis Mountains a few years back: "I consider one old cowboy worth more than a whole ship load of chinamens" or words to that effect. Furthermore, he spoke with the conviction of a man taking these words straight from the mouth of God himself. (In all fairness to the old feller, he had got fenced in with a couple of hundred head of horses and fifteen or twenty head of Chinese sailors on a slow boat to China one time. It was fun at first "but he had no idea them chinks talk so funny and eat sech funny grub or that Chiney was so damn fur off.")

Prejudice notwithstanding, inside that rough exterior dwelt a sentimental softie, toward horses same as toward women—if not more so. That is to say, he could be moved to tears by the courage and faithfulness of a horse as readily as he could the courage and faithfulness of a good woman. The following episode will bear this out:

Man or (in deference to women's lib) womankind alone does not control the corner on courage. Neither does he or she dominate the field in perseverance. Mance Bomar of Marfa tells of one Crescencio Sanchez (of Marathon) who was sent out on a Mexican pony to locate a bunch of wild mares so the other cowboys could come after them. Out of the question for Sanchez to fetch them—one man on a scroungy, gimlet-rumped Spanish pony that wouldn't weigh 750 pounds with a solid gold saddle on. All mane and tail, except he could boast an exceptionally big head and shoulders, which was nothing to boast about since neither enhanced his speed, endurance, or beauty.

Around one o'clock in the afternoon Sanchez spotted the bunch but, unluckily, the bunch spotted him. This meant he would have to stay with them, otherwise he might not locate them again for months. Suffice it to say that the bunch left there like so many arrows shot from a bow with little Mexico chomping and foaming at the bits to be one of the crowd.

Came sundown. Then dark. Then moonrise, with the herd still running strong and little bay Mexico not only still "buildin' to 'em" but faunching at the bits for more. As night wore on, the bunch sure must have begun to wonder what kind of two-headed, four-eyed, six-legged monster could this be? By this time the *manada* (mares, fillies, and their master, the stud horse) was leg-and-lung weary to the extent that Sanchez and little Mex set the direction.

Around daylight Sanchez and the little pony showed up at Arthur Mitchell headquarters with all except those critters that fell by the wayside from pure exhaustion. This after a run of what the boys calculated to be fully 150 miles, taking into account the distance from lower San Francisco Creek plus the countless meanderings required in an operation of this kind.

Shed of the saddle, little Mexico staggered off a few steps from the water trough, spraddled his front legs, dropped his head, and stood there, trembling. He was still standing there when Sanchez checked him at noon. He was standing there just before dark. Sanchez offered him a little water which he drank, and pitched him a little alfalfa which he ate. And his trembling had stopped. Even so, Sanchez expected him to be dead by morning. So, hugging the scrawny neck and patting the ungainly head he bade the little critter a final *adiós* and *vaya con Dios*. Oh, he of little faith! not to say poor judgment. Next morning, little Mexico was still on his feet though he hadn't untracked. About this time the horse jingler brought the *remuda* by. The little critter throwed his head up, nickered, and joined them, ready for another run through hell or through highwater or a combination thereof. (Here, little Mexico epitomizes what a noted and notorious infidel said a hundred years ago—I cannot recall his name—"It is not always the strength of the body or the brilliance of mind but the quality of the spirit that makes for greatness," or words to that effect.)

Every time I tell this tale (every time I get among old-time cowboys) it never fails to bring tears and wring hearts. Needless to say I join them. Right around on the other hand, nobody sheds a tear, myself included, when I tell of (re-tell, I should say) one tragic time I loved and lost, which, I suppose, tells you more about the old-time cowboy character than I intended to tell.

"This is John Patterson, year 1927 or '28, and the ranch is the 7h (called seven half h) of 120 sections lying partly in Crockett and Upton counties and owned by the late Monte Noelke (the first) of Mertzon. High Lonesome, the headquarters, lay 10 miles southeast of Rankin and Cedar Canyon, adjoining High Lonesome on the east and the Pecos River on the west. In the picture Pullwater has just fallen victim to my brother John's hoolihan loop. What my brother John must not know is he is fixin' to fall victim to Pullwater."

—Paul Patterson

The Gathering

by Marguerite Nixon

Along the Sabine River, where it borders Texas on the east, there is a territory that was once known as No Man's Land because of a controversy over whether it belonged to Mexico or the United States. It was a sanctuary, in a way, for criminals. Aaron Burr is said to have fled there after killing Alexander Hamilton in the duel, and the old Burr's Ferry was supposed to be a testament to his having been there.

But the outlaws came quickly and left quietly, for the settlers meant to have the black lands for their own. My father's people, the Tanners, settled there on a Mexican land grant. They were tall, blue eyed men who rode with engraved powder horns on their saddles and who knew a gun as intimately as a plow and liked it better. But so did their neighbors. A feud arose between the Tanners and the Hinsons over cattle, hogs, or horses. My father, who was eight or nine at the time, doesn't remember which, but it had to be one of these. They shared everything else—food, shelter, even clothing.

There had been no shooting as yet, possibly because a deer trail had not brought two men face to face. But the women had been ordered not to visit and the children were forbidden to meet and play together. My father missed Hines Hinson dreadfully. It was no fun going coon hunting by torchlight with only a pack of dogs for company, and he was the only other boy of that age within seven miles.

That's the way it had been all that fall, and now Christmas was almost at hand. It was the old custom to set up a community Christmas tree in the church house, and for some reason the preparations went on, although the whole settlement was uneasy.

The Tanner men cut an eight-foot long-leaf pine tree, dark green and bristling and fragrant, and set it up in front of the pews as usual, and the women and children of both factions came in stealthily, seeming to know when the others were absent, and trimmed it with paper chains, cotton balls, and tiny candles in tin clip-on candle holders.

The same procedure was used for bringing in gifts. Little packages began to fill up the branches. Braided ox whips and even a pair of deer antlers lay with name tags at the base of the tree. A string of beads made from dried chinaberries hung from a pine branch. All home-made gifts.

My grandfather was a wood worker; he etched and carved and smoothed wood into furniture and chests. On the farm was an old mule named Rufe, and he and my father were friends in the way that animals and children love one another. So my grandfather had carved a miniature of Rufe from a piece of weathered oak he'd found by the creek, and this he had placed on the tree as my father's Christmas gift.

As the preparations went on, the tension mounted. It was obvious that everyone was coming. No one intended to stay home that night. And the fear was that something dreadful would happen on Christmas Eve in the church yard, or even the church itself.

The church consisted of one room with two rows of rough, wooden pews, and at the end of the aisle stood the lectern holding the Bible and two kerosene lamps. There were no stained glass windows, but Grandma Hinson had made a sampler and hung it on the wall where all could see it. Stitched in red wool yarn were these words from St. Matthew: "For where two or three are gathered together in my name, there am I in the midst of them."

On Christmas Eve the people began to gather. They came on horseback and in wagons with hot bricks wrapped in quilts to keep them warm. It was a wonderful, cold, clear night with lots of stars and the tree spires reaching up to them. Even the little church sent out a warm glow from the two lighted lamps and the flickering Christmas tree candles. The only thing lacking was happiness and good will toward men.

It was rumored that one of the Hinsons had made a hangman's noose and wrapped it as a gift for one of the Tanners. If this were true, there would be a killing right then and there. Everyone waited apprehensively.

The Hinson family came in, grim-faced, and sat down, and the Tanners, just as grim, marched down the aisle and took their place in the opposite pews.

No one knew when the strange boy came in. He sat alone in the back of the church, his hands clasped in his lap. He was somewhere around twelve or fourteen years old. His dark hair was too long; even by pioneer standards he needed a hair cut. He looked straight ahead at the tree and Grandma Hinson's sampler.

Brother Fleming opened the Bible to Luke and read, "For unto you is born this day in the city of David, a Saviour, which is Christ the Lord." Then he told the old familiar story of how the Holy Family came into Bethlehem that night, Joseph walking and Mary riding the little donkey, and there was no room at the inn.

After that there was nothing left to do but start calling the names and handing out the presents. Brother Fleming's voice quavered as he read each name tag. Hines Hinson got a ten-cent Barlow knife. My father felt a deep pang because he thought he would never get to examine it.

And then his own name was called. He went forward to receive his gift and unwrapped it for all to see, as was the custom. It was Old Rufe, all right, long, flopping ears—gentle, plodding hooves.

And it could have been a replica of the tiny donkey that carried Mary that Holy Night. My father ran his thumbs over the miniature, and he looked up at the boy in the back of the room.

"He had the saddest eyes I've ever seen," my father said. And for some reason—"I've never known why," my father said, he held out his hand with the little carved mule and offered it to the strange boy. The boy came quietly down the aisle and accepted the gift.

Hines Hinson jumped up from his seat and ran up front where my father stood. "You gave him Old Rufe!" he exclaimed. But after a moment he said, "Well, that's all right. You can share my knife. You can keep it a week and I'll keep it a week."

The strange boy smiled then.

"His face shone brighter than the lamp," Grandma Hinson said.

In an instant, it seemed, joy filled the room. Like a breeze. Like a gentle wind upon the water. Like a spirit. It was Christmas Eve. Everybody was laughing and talking. The Tanners and Hinsons were slapping each other on the back. No one saw the strange boy leave. When they looked he was gone. They had been too busy exchanging gifts of crocheted garters and sleeve holders, jars of blackberry preserves and mayhaw jelly.

"Where'd that boy go?" my grandfather asked. He went to the church door to look. But there was not a sign, not a footprint.

"Where did he come from?"

"I bet he's from that family of squatters camped over at the old Kincaid place," an uncle said. "I'll ride over there tomorrow and take a look."

But they had not seen a black-haired boy. "Every one of those young'uns was redheaded as woodpeckers," my uncle said.

The boy was never seen again, not a trace. The only people who ever saw him at all were the ones inside the church that Christmas Eve. But one fact remains: there was never another feud in that particular section of the piney woods of East Texas.

Mildew on the Elephant Ears

by Al Lowman

In one of his comedies about life in Marseilles, French dramatist Marcel Pagnol has the principal character facing east. If he turns a quarter, he faces north; another quarter, west; and another, south. From this exercise, he concludes that if all four directions converge where he is standing, then Marseilles must indeed be located at the center of the earth. I have known people, using much the same logic, who thought that Staples was at the center of the earth.

Take, for example, Uncle Quincy, one of Daddy's older brothers who became a career law enforcement officer. In 1934 he was a freshman D.P.S. trooper assigned to state headquarters in Austin. During his first week of regular duty, his sergeant sent him on an official errand across town. The population of Austin at that time was sixty thousand, scarcely the metropolis it has since become. He was expected back well before noon. At five minutes to five that evening, Uncle Quince reappeared at headquarters looking worn but triumphant. He had had difficulty locating the address. The map in the glove compartment of his patrol car had done him no good whatever because he lacked any meaningful reference point. Suddenly, a fellow trooper standing nearby realized the problem. "Hell, sarge, he had to go forty miles to Staples to start!"

This is no isolated episode. Some half-dozen years ago the family was shocked to learn that Uncle Travis and his wife were going to Europe. There are, you see, certain of our relatives who react like that exotic Swiss wine that is alleged to turn sour whenever it is transported more than a short distance from its cellars. We still do not know how Aunt Clera persuaded him to ac-

87

company her on this trip. Since Uncle Travis suffers from acute acrophobia, his wife thought it peculiar that he insisted on sitting by the window on the port side of the plane. Nor did he shut his eyes during takeoff. Instead, he leaned forward and scanned the horizon with an intensity that approached anxiety. Finally he turned to his wife in despair and said, "I can't find Staples down there." He's been told that they went to London, Paris, Rome, and other places. But he won't swear to it because he never got oriented.

Staples folk can't be accused of not knowing their place. They struggle to stay in it. They also have a supremely clear view of themselves in relation to their neighbors at Martindale and Fentress. A couple of stories will illustrate. Last year at a social function in San Marcos I visited with Emmett Harper, formerly of Martindale. During our conversation Mr. Harper reminisced pleasantly about dirt-street days in the village of his youth. Back then, he recalled, Arthur Smith used to sprinkle the streets in summertime, using a mule-drawn water wagon. Later, I asked eighty-eight-year-old Bill Whitten if he remembered a similar service having been provided in Staples. He responded with a deadpan expression, even tone of voice, and not-too-subtle scorn, "Son, nobody *ever* watered down Staples!" So much for Martindale.

Fentress, in those days, was a resort town. Resort towns are a haven for people with time on their hands. An idle mind is the devil's workshop. Therefore, the folks in Fentress probably had more fun than they should have. They had a large pavillion where, on alternate nights, they would either roller-skate or *dance*! Admittedly, they might have danced to the tune of "Whispering Hope," but they danced nonetheless. I asked Cliett Lowman, Daddy's eighty-year-old cousin, if there had ever been any dancing in Staples. "LORD NO!" On recovering from the stupidity of my question, he added, "Why they'd a-churched you!"

About ten steps beyond the pavillion at Fentress was the bathhouse, which stood high on the riverbank. Let it be clearly understood that this bathhouse—with all its nooks, crannies, and dressing (or undressing) stalls—was strictly off limits at sundown.

If Staples residents thought theirs was the first rest stop on the road from the Garden of Eden, then it was equally apparent to them that Fentress was the first stop in the other direction. The Reverend Vasco Teer was the Methodist preacher in Staples from 1927 to 1930. One Sunday he delivered a scorching admonition to Staples parents on the folly of allowing their offspring to frequent Fentress. To hear him tell it, Fentress was where the devil vacationed when his place froze over. Edra Allbright (of San Marcos) grew

Above: The no-
torious Fentress
bathhouse, scene
of rendezvous
and revelry; *left*:
The Rev. V. W.
Teer, "How you
gonna keep 'em
in Staples after
they've seen Fen-
tress?"

up in Fentress. She was one of the Collier girls. Recently she told me that before Brother Teer even finished his sermon, several folks sneaked out of
the church and drove to Fentress to see how bad it was. Word of his warn
ing was spread the length of the upper San Marcos valley before noon that day.

For many years one of the most noted dissidents in that valley was O. H.
Gregg, an Episcopal bishop's son turned Republican. In 1913 he wrote about
valley life in the *Guadalupe Gazette,* recalling that on his arrival in 1867,
the whole country between Gonzales and San Marcos was devoid of settlement, except at Prairie Lea. There was no Staples then. Farming was con-
fined to river bottomland, and stock raising was the principal industry. Gregg
remembered that "if anyone wanted beef the neighbors would shoulder a
rifle, go out and kill a fat cow, [then hang] a quarter up in a tree, where
it could be had as long as any remained. It would keep in June, July, or
August as the air was pure. But," continued Gregg, "the people are so mean
now that the air is contaminated, and it would not keep twelve hours without
being well-salted."

Staples has never run dry of characters filled with advice or admonition.
Some were boarders in the Lowman family home; others hung around the
drugstore and post office. In the fall of 1896, Grandpapa's first cousin (once
removed) showed up from Alabama. Lowman Howard was the family's boarder
for twenty years, until he married grandmama's sister and established a home
of his own. He was grandpapa's bookkeeper and factotum. The Lowman boys
called him "Judge" and regarded him good-naturedly as the family's oracle.
Of medium build and height, he was bald as a cucumber, with a fringe of
greying hair above the ears, as I remember him. He also sported a Teddy
Roosevelt-style moustache, except that Judge's was more closely cropped. He
admired T. R. extravagantly, proclaiming him the greatest of all American
presidents.

Teddy Roozevelt—as Judge called him—was celebrated for his tremendous
vitality. Such was not the case with Lowman Howard. Back in Alabama his
daddy had a friend and neighbor who was wont to say, "I'm as fond of work
as the next fellow, but I'm not a fool about it." Lowman Howard wasn't a
fool about it either. In Staples, where the Protestant work ethic enjoyed
a considerable vogue, his approach to life was best compared to the old,
single-cylinder, hit-and-miss gasoline engine that some of us remember from
our childhood. The piston fired only when the momentum of the flywheel
had subsided to a preset level. That was Lowman Howard; he fired only when
he had to. Which wasn't often.

Left: Lowman Howard, at odds with Prohibition and the work ethic; *below*: Q. J. Lowman, Texas Ranger. Asked what the initials stood for, he replied, "Quick Justice."

It was an open secret that Judge loved his beer, but in prohibitionist Staples, this was socially inconvenient. He addressed the problem by stashing his brew in the river at the pumphouse. He took upon himself the responsibility of going there one or more times each day to grease the gears. His devotion to duty was exemplary. It summoned him at the most unlikely hours. He would pull the watch from his vest pocket, study the face intently, then solemnly announce, "Time to grease the pump." It was a ploy accepted only by the blissfully naive and the doggedly innocent.

Like most of us, Lowman Howard had a capacity for misattributing cause and effect. About 1930, two nephews, Quince and Travis Lowman, took him to San Antonio where its baseball team was to play Tulsa's. Quince had thoughtfully packed away a cooler filled with Pearl beer expressly for Judge's pleasure. By the time they reached San Antonio, Judge was well oiled.

Seated in Mission Stadium, in a vast sea of home team boosters, Judge decided that the visitors needed his support. Whenever they were in a position to score, he would wobble to his feet and holler, "C'mon Toolsy!" This made the chaperones nervous. Uneasiness grew when, after the game, Judge had to be assisted to the car. Sizing up the situation, the trip sponsors decided that he was too drunk to be deposited on his doorstep. So they made an unscheduled stop at an all-night diner, hopefully to sober him with a bit of food.

"What'll you have, Judge?" "Bring me a bowl of chili, the biggest you got!" He proceeded to eat lustily. The next morning he showed up at the post office, where all the hangers-on knew what had happened the previous evening. "How're ya doin' this morning, Judge?" Quince asked solicitously. "I'll tell ya, Q," he admitted ruefully, "that bowl of red like to got me last night."

Soon after Lowman Howard arrived in the fall of ninety-six, there came Ann Vanderber, the family's housekeeper and faithful friend, whose origins remained shrouded in mystery until the day she died thirty-two years later. For example, the 1900 census says she was born in Arkansas, the 1910 census says Tennessee, and her obituary in 1928 says Missouri.

Lowman Howard and Ann Vanderber, like so many others in Staples, had advice to give. Judge used to proclaim "It's cheaper to re-elect the incumbent; he's already got his pockets stuffed." This might be true, only if one assumes that human avarice has its limits. Miss Vanderber's counsel was, "Never tell a woman anything you don't want told; sooner or later, she'll tell it." Miss Vanderber recalled making this statement at an Ozark quilting party in the 1860s. A dour-faced mountain woman seated nearby contemplated the statement a moment, then announced drily, "That's a lie; I killed my husband thirty years ago, and I never told a soul!"

Another of Staples' best-remembered characters was Marvin Scott, Grandmama's brother, an unlicensed druggist and sometimes postmaster. Although not a member of the household, he was the much-loved confidant from whom the boys learned not only the facts of life, but also the facts of living. Uncle Marvin was a preacher's son whose thought processes were uniquely his own. He might, for example, contemplate the New Testament stricture that lusting in the heart is tantamount to performing the act. From this premise he would advance to the conclusion that to think about dropping a five-dollar bill in the collection plate was as good as doing it. (That kind of logic goes right over the heads of most preachers.) One can be certain that Marvin Scott knew his way around Fentress. In his worldly outlook, virtue would have held no meaning unless one were acquainted with the alternatives.

Besides, Mark Twain had a valid point when he remarked that the list of sins for which people could go to hell was so extensive that trying to save them seemed scarcely worth the effort. Even so, Methodists at Staples made that effort, especially during their protracted meeting held in late July. The campgrounds were across the river in a giant pecan grove, and no meeting was ever considered finished until Lewey Lowman (Grandpapa's youngest brother) and his best friend Cumby Vinyard (the local barber) came forward to be saved. This annual event occurred at the final Sunday service, after which Lewey and Cumby would go out and celebrate their redemption with an evening of sobriety.

Alcohol was available to local Prohibitionists in the form of Peruna, obtainable at Cramer's Store. Peruna was advertised as "Dr. Hartman's World Renowned Catarrh Medicine." It was twenty-eight percent alcohol. Staples must have been the catarrh capital of Texas; Cramer became relatively prosperous selling the stuff. Great-grandpa Harmon Lowman had his own nonalcoholic recipe for curing catarrh, a recipe that has been preserved in his Bible. Oddly enough, one of the ingredients is carbolic acid. My pharmacist friend speculates that its purpose was to cauterize the lungs. It would put an end to catarrh, all right.

Lewey Lowman had no use for piety, pretense, or prohibition. Indeed, he viewed them each with regal disregard. Possibly all of this was a reaction to the unbending rectitude of his father, a farmer and schoolteacher who preached when given the opportunity. And if he wasn't given it, he sometimes

Left: Marvin Scott, always consistent in his logic; *right*: Lewey Lowman, no use for piety, pretense, or Prohibition.

took it. Any minister foolish enough to call on old Harmon for a benediction was inviting rebuttal to the sermon just concluded. It says in the Book of Romans that the wages of sin is death, but when Grandpa Harmon prayed, the wages of righteousness was a late dinner in every Methodist home in Staples. And that was most of them.

That dinner generally featured fried chicken. Johnny Vinyard, grandmama's 102-year-old cousin, explains: "People then didn't have much refrigeration, so meat had to be eaten before it spoiled. You weren't supposed to handle a fishing pole or a gun on Sunday, but it was all right to run down a chicken and wring its neck by hand. It had the same result for the chicken, but it made Papa feel better." Johnny Vinyard, it might be noted, was another who cared little for pretense.

In addition to their religious underpinnings, some of the family members paid obeisance to certain superstitions as a means of thwarting evil in day-to-day living. Aunt Evie, arthritic at eighty, can still chunk a mean rock at any hoot owl that perches outside her bedroom window as a harbinger of death. Even on sweltering summer nights, she lies abed, windows raised, air conditioner turned off, just to listen for little hooty owls. Aunt Ila never set a table until all of the guests had arrived safely under her roof. To do otherwise would invite bad luck upon host and visitors alike. Daddy had his own superstition. He believed that voting Republican would lead to economic downturn, mounting unemployment, widespread business failures, falling commodity prices, and wholesale foreclosures on farm and ranch property.

Daddy was a brass-collar Methodist and a devout Democrat. Staples had, and still has, many others like him. The morning after Reagan's election in 1980, I went to visit Johnny Vinyard, then on the eve of his one-hundredth birthday. "What did you think of the election, Mr. Johnny?" He reacted instantaneously, one might say reflexively. "Son, we're blowed up!" Centenarians, as a rule, don't have to rely on prophecy.

In conclusion, let me just say that what has happened before has happened once again. Each time I've written one of these papers about Staples, I've drawn up an outline. Each time, the stories start to crowd in until the outline is pushed out of sight. I vote with Peter Quennell, whose new book, *Customs and Characters*, makes this point: "To be remembered, talked over, perhaps even sometimes laughed at, is surely the only tribute that the dead require."

All photographs reproduced by permission of Al Lowman.

William N. Stokes, Sr., a Baptist deacon, among other things.

Forty-two Baptist Kids and Three Baptist Deacons

THE SAGA OF A "CHURCHING"

by William N. Stokes, Jr.

I n the early 1920s my father, William Stokes, was a practicing lawyer, also county attorney, in Vernon, Wilbarger County, Texas. He was a prominent leader in the First Baptist Church, a member of the board of deacons, a former superintendent of the Sunday school, a son of the church's former pastor, and a teacher of the church's largest class—sixty teenage girls.

It was in this last position that he became embroiled in a bitter brawl with the church hierarchy. At this time the nation was entering the Roaring Twenties. World War I was history, but its influences struck at all elements of the society. The teenage kids especially were affected. These young people were not impressed by the stern Victorian concepts of modesty, strict discipline, and full-time attention to affairs of the church and Sunday school. Likely, they were as "good" and "moral" as their bewildered parents had been at their age, but the direction of this morality had changed. The approach was more permissive, more liberal, more experimental.

These changes were reflected particularly in the kids' recreational activities. And nowhere was this more manifest than in changes that came in the dance. For whereas their predecessors moved gracefully and sedately to the waltz, the two-step, the square, and folk dances, the modern youngsters were swinging with the bunnyhug, foxtrot, fleahug, tango, and, a bit later, the Charleston. The Vernon kids adopted these new steps with enthusiasm, and many of those in the Judge's (for hereafter we shall so identify him, as later he did

97

become a trial and appellate judge) Sunday school class were squarely in the center of it all.

Soon these wicked goings-on attracted the attention of the pastor of the Baptist Church, Brother Ballard. The catalyst was an item in the town newspaper that gave a detailed account of a big shindig at the country club, complete with a list of those who were involved. Seventeen of the Judge's girls were named, as were twenty-five boys, all listed on the church rolls. Brother Ballard and Brother McGregor worked up a full boil on this wickedness and plunged immediately into action. The newspaper clip went onto the table at a meeting of the board of deacons, and Brother Ballard warmed to his task. "It's a violation of the laws of the church for members to dance. We have a duty to God and the church to meet this issue four-square. I recommend that the chair appoint two committees, one of good men in the church who will talk to the boys, another of good women who will talk with the girls. The errants will be advised that they must attend the next prayer meeting, apologize publicly to the church for their sin, and promise never to repeat it. Failing this, they must be removed from the membership rolls of the church."

The brothers around the table were silent, but at length a motion was made that the recommendations be approved and executed. The motion passed, the committees were designated, and a motion to adjourn was made. But at this point the Judge intervened: "A foolish and ill-advised move. The kids will not show up at a prayer meeting or any other public session, much less apologize. Given this choice, they will leave the church. What you are doing is separating the church from a large segment of its best and most promising young people. They will live with such an experience to their dying days, and many of them may never return to the church rolls. Furthermore, you have no authority to take this action. Deacons in the Baptist Church have no disciplinary powers. Their function is simply to advise the congregation, which is the sole repository of power and authority. But of even more significance, we have—as all of us know well—a number of grown-ups in our congregation who drink liquor, chase women; many play cards, yes, and many dance. If these last two be sins at all, surely they are less serious than many of the others; yet here we are singling out and threatening the youngsters and letting the elders off scot-free."

This speech was greeted by long stares and a heavy silence, after which the meeting adjourned. The following day the Judge was summoned by Brother McGregor, the deacons' chairman. He characterized the Judge's remarks as a revolt against the established authority of the church. He was disturbed that a member of the board of deacons would interfere with the imposition of essential church discipline. The Judge repeated his points; Brother McGregor was not impressed.

A week passed, and the chairman called a special meeting of the board. Here Pastor Ballard gave a lecture on church discipline and on the importance of its enforcement. "The church has no greater enemy than the dance, an institution created by the devil for his own nefarious purposes. Our errant Brother Stokes here is defending the dance and thereby striking at the very heart of church discipline."

"Not at all," answered the Judge. "I do not defend the dance as such, though I find it much less of a sin (if a sin at all) than many believe it. What I ask is that we change our disciplinary approach. We must recognize that we live in changing times. Women have shortened their skirts and bobbed their hair. They ride astride on horseback, and I am told that in some parts of the country they even smoke cigarettes. We must recognize that our young people are in the very heart of these changes and are attempting to adjust to them. We should approach them in a spirit of love, charity, and understanding rather than accuse them as criminals and threaten them with prosecution and humiliation."

Brother Ballard sprang again to the attack. "Brethren, we cannot temporize on this. What we have is a festering cancer within the body of the church. If these young people will not make public confession and apology, we must remove them from our midst." Brother Ballard then suggested that guidance of the Lord be sought, and he asked Brother Oates (a friendly deacon) to lead in prayer. And he instructed Brother Oates, "Ask the Lord to give special guidance to Brother Stokes."

Some weeks passed. It became obvious that Brother Ballard and his associates were stymied in getting at the kids as long as Brother Stokes was in the way. He was a skilled lawyer, but more important, he was schooled in theory and fact of the fundamental doctrines of the Baptist Church. He used these weapons effectively, and the brothers were frustrated and angry.

But the brothers also were ingenious. They were not without cunning, and they decided to regroup and pursue another tack. The waters were allowed to calm, and at length the Judge was gratified that perhaps the controversy would die. This feeling seemed to be confirmed by a significant development. The pastor announced that a revival meeting two weeks in length was to be held. Brother Clapp, a former minister of the Vernon Church would bring the messages. The Judge loved Brother Clapp, who now was pastor of the Baptist Church in Palestine, Texas.

The revival began on a high note. Brother Clapp brought a number of inspiring sermons. In the course of the revival, however, the Judge was disturbed to learn from Brother Clapp that on his induction as pastor in Palestine he faced a serious situation. Many of the membership were disloyal or disinterested. Many were boozers, womanizers, hell-raisers in general, yet they retained active membership. Brother Clapp told the Judge in detail how he had solved this problem. He had gathered the genuine Christian leaders of the church around him, and together they had made an end run. It had been announced that a new church covenant would be submitted to the congregation for adoption. Here the fundamental tenets of the church (including vows to abstain from boozing, woman-chasing, hell-raising) were reaffirmed. All members would sign the covenant; those not signing would no longer be members. Thus Brother Clapp had adroitly purged the membership rolls of the unworthies, and the church went its way and prospered.

The Vernon revival moved to its conclusion. At the end of one of the later sessions, Brother Ballard announced that a "convention" would be held after the services. He suggested meaningfully that all visitors and noninterested members were free to leave. Less than a hundred remained, made up primarily of the faithful sympathizers and allies of Brother Ballard and his group. Brother Ballard then announced that the deacons had prepared a new church covenant, the text of which was as follows:

> BE IT RESOLVED, that the covenant be revised and amended as follows: henceforth we as members and Christians shall not and will not countenance as members of the Church those who drink, gamble, play cards, dance or attend dances, card parties, theaters, picture shows or other places of sin and worldly amusement.

Brother Ballard asked for a motion to adopt the covenant, which promptly was made and seconded. Here the Judge arose. He emphasized the serious nature of adopting a new covenant. He suggested that this one obviously was hastily prepared and loosely drafted. Example: "those who drink." Drink *what?* Water? Soda pop? Milk? Of course the deacons must have had intoxicating liquor in mind, but why didn't they say so? The Judge then pointed to the success of Brother Clapp's revival and suggested that this was a disturbing interruption that should be considered in later times. He moved to table the motion to adopt the covenant.

Brother Ballard was frantic. He ruled the motion to table out of order. The Judge retorted promptly that a motion to table was always in order; moreover, it was not debatable—and he cited Robert's *Rules of Order* in support. After more hesitation and confusion Brother Ballard had to put the motion to table, and it passed sixty-six to eleven. The "convention" adjourned. In all the hubbub even the usual benediction was omitted.

The following morning the Judge had a visit from Brother Clapp. He expressed embarrassment that he had been used. He supported the Judge's position and apologized for being involved, even though he had had no previous knowledge of the purposes and motives behind his invitation to conduct the revival. He recognized the substantial differences between his situation in Palestine and that of the Vernon church. In Palestine it was the big folks, the so-called church leaders, who were involved. In Vernon these elements were pushed under the rug, and the full force of the church was thrown against a group of helpless youngsters.

The revival concluded, and things remained quiet a few weeks. Once again the Judge visualized that perhaps the controversy was at an end. But on a Sunday morning Brother Ballard chose for his text some verses from Paul's letter to the Corinthians in which divisions among members of the church at Corinth were described. Brother Ballard preached for more than an hour, ending with a dramatic peroration. "Brethren, on an occasion similar to this some years ago I stood on one foot (the other was infected) and preached a sermon an hour and fifteen minutes in length, preparing my church to turn out a deacon, his wife, and his daughter."

BLOOEY!! The lines were drawn. An ominous new note was injected. Here were six-guns at dawn. For the first time the Judge suspected that *he*, not the kids, was the primary target.

The Judge knew he had allies, and he sought them out. He counted two major church leaders in his corner. One was Brother Hockersmith. Let the Judge describe him:

> He was a deacon in the Church. A man of rather small stature, a ruddy face overshadowed by a shock of white hair, shaggy eyebrows of the same hue, from under which gleamed a pair of steel-blue eyes which seemed to say that their owner had serious doubts as to the truth and accuracy of the things you were saying. His legs were bowed, shoulders slightly stooped, and he looked at you with an expression that he did not give a rip or a rap what you or anyone else thought of him. He loved his friends and despised his enemies, who always were 100% wrong; and their wrongness always stemmed from iniquitous motives.

The other ally was Brother Foster, a retired Baptist minister. He was a persuasive talker, an influential peacemaker who in the beginning of the controversy cultivated both sides in an effort to defuse the explosion. Now he concluded that the pastor and deacons were pushing it too far, and he sided with the defense.

Quickly it developed that Brother Foster knew much of the machinations of the pastor and deacons. After hesitations and false starts he finally bluntly confirmed that the charges were to be brought against the Judge at the forthcoming prayer meeting. The proceedings were to be brought to conclusion by vote of those present. No notice would be given the Judge or anyone else; it would be a "surprise party." The Judge was overwhelmed. "Charges—against ME?" "Yes, YOU," Brother Foster continued. "They have their minds made up, and I don't believe there's anything you or anyone else can do about it. They've concluded they'll never be able to do anything with those young people about attending dances as long as you are a member of the church, and they will have to get rid of you first. And, of course, at a Wednesday night prayer meeting, where only their own cohorts and allies attend, they likely will have the votes."

Thus the gauntlet was hurled. After long contemplation and soul-searching the Judge concluded, "I have but one thing left to do, a dramatic and serious step, but they have left me with no choice." As indicated earlier, the Judge was county attorney of Wilbarger County. He was aware of the things going on in the community, and one of the institutions that "went on" was a weekly poker game at a rod-and-gun club in the north end of the county. Stakes often were high, and the players pushed their cards through the night into the early, and sometimes the late, hours of the morning. One of the most active participants in these games was the chairman of the board of deacons of the First Baptist Church, Brother McGregor—yes, the same Brother McGregor who backed Brother Ballard to the hilt in efforts to "church" the kids for dancing and who now was ready to ride out the Judge for interfering with the process.

The following morning the Judge convened a hearing known as a "court of inquiry." This was and is held before a justice of the peace and is designed to inquire into and ferret out violations of the law. Now at that time in Texas, playing cards in a public place, even an innocent game of bridge, was a violation of the law; and gambling in *any* place, public or private, was outlawed and severe penalties were imposed.

The Judge got out subpoenas to two citizens. They were brought to court, granted immunity from prosecution (thereby forcing them to testify), and placed on the witness stand. Both men testified that, yes, they *had* played poker the previous Tuesday night at the rod-and-gun club; money in substantial sums was at stake; and, yes, Brother McGregor was an active participant throughout the night and early into the next morning. Whereupon Brother McGregor was hauled into court. On being confronted with the charges and the testimony of his fellow-gamblers, he meekly entered a plea of guilty and paid his fine.

The town was electrified. Yet even with their ranks depleted by the loss of Brother McGregor's influence, the pastor and deacons proceeded with their charges against the Judge at prayer meeting. Although he had information of these plans from Brother Foster, the Judge had no official notice or information that the charges were to be pursued at this session. Brothers Hockersmith and Foster had no notice either that—surprise!—they too now were added as defendants. They also were to be "churched," and a motion to accomplish this was made.

Once again the Judge took the platform. He pointed out that the charges were brought without notice to him or the others. Indeed, his two co-defendants were not even present. This was a violation of every principle of Anglo-Saxon justice. Surely in the United States of America, in the State of Texas, they would not haul people up in court to try and convict them on only ten minutes' notice, with two of them absent in the bargain! This made sense to a majority at the prayer meeting, and the trial was postponed to a later date—two weeks, this time before the congregation.

On a hot summer night the trial was held in the tabernacle, an open-air structure adjoining the church. Vernon had never seen anything like this. Under the roof of the tabernacle were the church members; on a wide expanse of grass in the rear was the rest of the town. Estimates were that 3,500 people attended. Brother Mason, a key conspirator, was named prosecutor. Witnesses testified in broad and general terms, without specifics, that the Judge interfered with imposition of church discipline. No testimony whatever implicated Brothers Hockersmith and Foster. The defense put on no witnesses.

Then came the summation. The Judge took the podium in his own defense. The other two, he pointed out, needed no defense since no evidence had been developed against them. His speech was more than an hour in length. He went over the facts in detail and explained his position. He replied to the only real criticism leveled against him, that of hauling Brother McGregor to court for gambling. This, it was hinted, was going a bit too far. Here he went dramatically into his position—facing alone (as he then thought) a prayer meeting kickout. His defense was spirited, complete—and effective.

Came time for the vote; a secret ballot was ruled out; nonmembers might vote. The call was made for those who favored disciplining the three defendants to stand. Twenty-six members stood to their feet. At this point Brother Hockersmith arose, pencil and tablet poised, and requested the voters "to remain standing a moment while I take down your names." Those opposing dismissal then were called. A hundred and forty-six arose. The trial was over.

At the conclusion Brother Ballard rushed to Mr. Hockersmith and gushed, "I'm for you, Brother Hockersmith." Brother Hockersmith sneered and turned his back. Thereafter, for the remainder of his life, he spoke not a word to Brother Ballard or to anyone on his list who had voted against him. He darkened the doors of the Baptist Church not at all as long as Brother Ballard was pastor—which, incidentally, was not a great length of time after these events transpired. Rebuffed by Brother Hockersmith, Brother Ballard approached the Judge and offered his hand, which the Judge accepted, and the two embraced. The matter was closed. The Judge, Brother Foster, Brother Hockersmith, and the forty-two kids remained on the church rolls. "Many of these youngsters," the Judge concluded, "today are among the staunchest, most active, and influential members of the First Baptist Church of Vernon."

Old Army Went to Hell in 1958

AGGIE WAR STORIES FROM THE CORPS OF CADETS

by Joe S. Graham

Almost everyone is acquainted with that ubiquitous form of Aggie folklore, the Aggie Joke. There is another genre of folk narrative, however, that is practically unknown outside Aggieland, or even outside the Corps of Cadets. These narratives I have tentatively called "War Stories" for reasons that will become apparent.

When I was in the graduate program at the University of Texas in 1975, an article appeared in the *Daily Texan*, the import of which was great puzzlement over the "Aggie Spirit." This "Aggie Spirit," including the seemingly obsessive concern with bonfires and other traditions, is difficult for newcomers to Texas A & M to understand. A number of my colleagues in the Department of English are perplexed and some even put off by the seemingly fanatic commitment to "tradition" at A & M—not only among students but also among some faculty and administration. In this paper I shall attempt, in anthropological and folkloristic terms, to account for this Aggie Spirit, especially in the Corps, and I shall attempt to assess the role that a certain type of folklore—Aggie War Stories—plays in this sense of belonging and pride.

The Corps of Cadets, until 1963 compulsory for the first two years of a student's career, continues to exert an influence on the student body disproportionate to its size: some two thousand Corps members out of an enrollment of slightly over thirty-six thousand students. The Corps is the most conservative element on campus and has taken on the role of guardian of the traditions of the school. This role is not just a historical one; it is also an inevitable one. To understand the Aggie Spirit, one must understand the Corps of Cadets. And to understand the impact that the Corps experience has on a stu-

Aggie! (*Reproduced by permission of TAMU Archives*)

dent, one must understand the freshman experience in the Corps—it is pivotal to becoming an Aggie in the Corps. Although they may never admit it (though some will), many members of the Corps see themselves as the "true Aggies."[1]

The Corps is organized into military units—outfits—and each outfit is organized along military lines. Freshmen are organized into squads of from four to six fish, with a squad leader (a junior) and two assistant squad leaders (sophomores). Several squads make up a company, and companies are organized into larger units. The most intense interactions occur on the squad and company levels.

Unlike the armed services, the military rank of these cadet officers is less important than their classification. Freshmen are at the bottom of the social order and power structure and are subject (in varying degrees) to the control of all upperclassmen. The upperclassmen who exercise the most immediate control over the freshmen as a group are the sophomores, who look upon themselves as the disciplinarians of the outfit and who have the special charge of making an Aggie out of each freshman and insuring his transition from "high school hairy" to responsible adult and future leader.[2] Juniors preside not only over the sophomores but also over the freshmen, and seniors preside over everyone. It has been said that a senior in the Corps of Cadets has more power—more absolute control over others—than he will likely ever have again in his life.

The freshman year in the Corps can best be understood in terms of Arnold van Gennep's concept of the Rites of Passage, which he defined as rites that mark and ease every change of place, state, social position, and age.[3] The change involved in this case involves a change of status and social position, from high school senior into Aggie, a move from youth to manhood.

Rites of Passage consist of three phases: 1) rites of separation, 2) rites of transition, and 3) rites of reincorporation. The first phase, the rites of separation, comprises symbolic behavior signifying the detachment of the individual from an earlier fixed point in the social structure and cultural condition. For the high school graduate who is not going to college, graduation marks a movement from dependent to independent status, from one set of expectations (parents pay for everything, children remain obedient to parents) to another (free from parental authority but obligated to make one's own way in the world as an adult). For the high school graduate going to college, however, high school graduation marks the end of one social status and the beginning of another. For a Corps freshman, the separation marks a most dramatic change: he goes from being the top dog in high school to occupying the absolute bottom of the social structure—he may be required to address even animals and inanimate objects as "Sir" and "Mister." In the process, he is stripped of all his symbols of status and power—his distinctive clothing, haircut, automobile, etc.

The second phase in Rites of Passage, the marginal or liminal phase, is the rites of transition. According to Victor Turner, the ritual subject (the freshman in the Corps) in this phase "passes through a cultural realm that has few or none of the attributes of the past or coming state."[4] A freshman in the Corps has neither the status he had as a high school senior nor the status and power he will have even as a sophomore in the Corps. He is in a state of transition.

In the third and final phase, reincorporation, the passage is complete. Turner writes:

> The ritual subject is in a relatively stable state once more, and by virtue of this, has rights and obligations vis-à-vis others of a clearly defined and "structural" type; he is expected to behave in accordance with certain customary norms and ethical standards binding on incumbents of social position in a system of such positions.[5]

At the end of the freshman year, the Aggie must change much of his behavior. As a fish, his "privileges" are what he can get away with, and irresponsible behavior is not unexpected. He can violate rules in a way that seniors cannot, or at least with far fewer consequences. But as he becomes an upperclassman, he is no longer free of status, or of the connected obligations. As a matter of fact, Final Review at the end of his freshman year clearly marks, symbolically as well as factually, that change in status. Let us examine this ritualized ceremony, the rites of reincorporation.

Final Review is the last march-by of the year, the last time in a given year that the troops must Pass in Review before the military leaders at the university, before the president, and before the invited dignitaries and families of the students. Unlike other reviews, Final Review involves two separate march-bys. During the first Pass in Review, the Corps marches in the order it has all year—individuals occupy the same ranks and roles and statuses. At the end of the first march-by there is an interlude and then a second march-by. During this interlude, the seniors drop out, no more members of the Corps of Cadets—a bittersweet experience. Each of the other classes moves into the place it will occupy the following year. During this time, freshmen change the symbols that have marked them as freshmen and don those that they will wear as sophomores the following school year: they trade the cap with no braid for a cap with black braid; they remove the black cotton belt with a small buckle and replace it with a black nylon belt with a larger buckle; they remove the flat brass, which they have found so hard to keep looking good, and replace it with curved brass, which they have customized. Meanwhile, the sophomores exchange the black-braided cap for a white-braided cap, the black nylon belt for a white cotton belt. The juniors exchange the white-braided cap for a gold-and-black-braided cap, the white cotton belt for a white nylon belt with a buckle of stacked brass, and they don the symbol par excellence of the senior in the Corps of Cadets—the senior boots.

At the end of this interlude, the Corps again passes in review, this time with the new order in place: next year's cadet officers lead the march, and there are no longer any freshmen, even though this is a week before final exams and two weeks before graduation. In the eyes of the Corps, they are no longer freshmen. Prior to the interlude between passbys, a freshman was called "fish," he addressed another freshman (at least in the presence of upperclassmen) as "Fish Doe," and he called an upperclassman "Mr. Doe, Sir." During the interlude, freshmen begin "dropping handles" with each other and with upperclassmen. This involves a ritual, initiated by the freshmen-now-become-sophomores, in which a first-name-basis, and more egalitarian interaction, begins.[6] This brief ritual reaffirms the freshman's new status. He has assumed the role he will occupy for the next year, holding all the privilege and power and status of a sophomore.

Having briefly examined the three phases of the Rites of Passage, let us return to the experience of the freshman year in the Corps. The metamorphosis from "high school hairy" to Texas Aggie is a difficult and often painful experience, psychologically as well as physically. In spite of its difficulty, the year is often seen in retrospect as one of the happiest, most carefree of one's years at Aggieland. This seems paradoxical, but when former classmates meet in social situations, the topic they will most likely discuss is their freshman year experiences. And indeed, I have heard and collected far more stories about the freshman year than about any other experience.

Freshmen in the Corps have no status—they are in a liminal or marginal state, a state of betwixt and between, being neither "high school hairies" nor Aggies in the fullest sense.[7] A person who drops out of the Corps and/or Texas A & M during his freshman year is not an Aggie. If he drops out or flunks out during his sophomore year (or after) and eventually graduates

elsewhere, he may still consider himself an Aggie, and his former fish buddies may still think of him as an Aggie. To be *most* meaningful, that freshman
year should be spent in the corps dorms. "Day ducks," as day students in
the Corps are known, are looked upon with a bit of condescension because
they do not have to endure what the dorm freshmen have to endure as a
matter of course—the things fish in the dorms of the Aggie Corps of Cadets
go through on a daily basis. Day Ducks go home after classes and live ordi-
nary lives; dorm students continue their Aggie experience every waking hour.
This freshman year is a nine-month initiation, a Rite of Passage between
childhood and adulthood.

In high school, seniors are at the top of the social heap. They hold the
power and status vis-à-vis other students. Symbols of this status and power
are abundant—letter jackets and sweaters, senior rings, the popular dress
and grooming styles, automobiles, girlfriends. When the Corps-bound high
school senior arrives at A & M, he must shed these symbols of status and
power. He becomes just like all other Corps freshmen; his uniform is identical to all other freshman uniforms—except for one shoulder patch that
identifies the branch of service he has entered. A Corpsman can recognize
a freshman as far as he can see the uniform: cap with no braid; black cotton
belt with small buckle; flat brass. His haircut, especially, sets him apart from
upperclassmen. Instead of the long, flowing locks of high school days, he
is shorn, like Samson, and the haircut is *UGLY*. Its only redeeming value
is that it is easy to groom. Small comfort!

I remember my squad leader's laughingly telling the story of one of his
fish buddies when he went to get his initiatory haircut at the Memorial Student Center barbershop. As he sat in the chair and as the barber pushed
the clippers through the long, wavy red hair (cut in the ducktail of the 1950s),
he wept real tears. The victim also chuckled at the memory.

The freshman is constantly reminded of his lack of status and power in
his social interactions with fellow Corpsmen. He must "hit a brace"—or "pop
to"— and "whip out"—that is, stand at stiff attention and introduce himself
thus: "Howdy. Fish Jones is my name, Sir." Any upperclassman is to be
addressed as "Mr. Doe, Sir." The freshman must so recognize each upperclassman present and even run down the dorm hall to identify someone (or
to introduce himself to someone he doesn't know). Woe be unto a freshman
who does not speak to an upperclassman or who calls the upperclassman
by the wrong name!

We think of one's room as private space; a man's home is his castle, where he is king. In the Corps, it is a senior privilege to lock one's door while in the room. Whereas freshmen must knock before entering an upperclassman's room, all upperclassmen can unceremoniously enter a freshman's "hole" (freshmen do not have rooms) at will, any time of the day or night. When an upperclassman enters the room, all freshmen present must snap-to and shout, "Howdy, Mr. Doe, Sir." The only exception is when an upperclassman of equal or higher rank—i.e., classification—is already present. In such cases, the freshman greets the upperclassman without coming to attention.

As with his clothing and grooming, the freshman's "hole" is simple, even spartan. It is not a freshman privilege to have a carpet, a stereo, a refrigerator, or any other of an assortment of luxuries available to the upperclassman. One can take comfort only in the fact that, in time, his turn will come.

Perhaps more critical to the sense of powerlessness and absence of status is the fact that fish in the Corps are absolutely at the command, beck, and call of every upperclassman, day or night (except for "call to quarters," a time set aside for study during the evenings). The fish is confronted with a situation in which a young man only one year older—or perhaps even the same age—has such authority over him. And he must submit with at least outward humility. He is not allowed to talk back or to laugh ("buzz").

A freshman who screws up on any of a myriad of duties or who fails in any of a great number of mostly trivial tasks may be punished in any of a number of ways: performing push-ups, sitting on the little pink stool (the freshman sits as if on a little stool, with his back against the wall and his legs bent at the knees at a ninety-degree angle, with no support for his bottom), doing sweat-outs in the shower, shining shoes, waxing floors, etc. If he dares to smile, and gets caught, he must "knock the buzz off" by slapping his forehead with the palm of his hand and bumping the back of his head against the wall, and he then must pull his hand down over his face to "wipe the buzz off."

These and a number of other reminders of the fish's lack of status and power make up a way of life designed to reduce the high school senior from his former position of minor diety to that of an absolute zero, defined as the "lowest form of life." And the fish cannot even take comfort in his suffering. Sophomores of every class constantly harp on the fact that they are not permitted to harass the freshmen as they themselves had been harassed the year before. I began my freshman year in September of 1959, and I have heard innumerable times since, from Corpsmen who were sophomores dur-

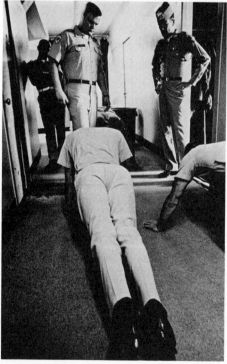

Above: Freshman cadet learning the Aggie tradition; *left*: Freshman cadet learning discipline (*Reproduced by permission of TAMU Archives*)

ing that year: "Ole Army went to hell in 1958, after our freshman year"—thus the title of this essay.

The only upperclassmen who cannot exercise this absolute power over freshmen is the "frog"—an upperclassman who has "frogged," or transferred into the Corps without going through the freshman year. Since he has not suffered through this period of initiation, he is not permitted to exercise power over freshmen.

Victor Turner's description of the second phase of Rites of Passage—the transition phase or marginal phase—is accurate for the freshman year in the Corps, although he based his observations on Ndembu religious rituals in Africa. He describes the initiate [at Texas A & M, the freshman] as follows:

> As liminal beings, they have no status, property, insignia, secular clothing indicating rank or role, position in a [kinship] system—in short, nothing that may distinguish them from their fellow neophytes or initiands. Their behavior is normally passive or humble; they must obey their instructors [upperclassmen] implicitly, and accept arbitrary punishment without complaint. It is as though they are being reduced or ground down to a uniform condition to be fashioned anew and endowed with additional powers to enable them to cope with their new station in life. Among themselves, neophytes tend to develop an intense comradeship and egalitarianism. Secular distinctions of rank and status disappear or are homogenized.[8]

The constant pressure and harassment, coupled with the sense of powerlessness, results in a profound sense of community among the freshmen, a sense of unity that Turner called *communitas*. This sense of community will continue long after the Aggie graduates and is no longer at the very heart of what has come to be known as the Aggie Spirit.

But the conditions under which freshmen must live are potentially explosive. The conformity expected of freshmen, along with the constant harassment, leads to frustrations that need an outlet. And indeed, there is a pressure valve to release the pressure before the possible explosion. Freshmen's experiences with this pressure-valve mechanism are the basis for one of the most frequently told types of Aggie War Stories.

If an upperclassman (or more often, two sophomores) singles out a freshman (or two freshmen roommates) for seemingly undeserved harassment, there are socially acceptable ways of evening the score and getting the upperclassman off the freshman's back. Of course, one always has the prerogative of inviting the offending upperclassman to the gym to put on boxing gloves. Yet this is a stated prerogative, an ideal that is never, to my knowledge, used in practice.

In spite of official, institutional disapproval, the retaliatory measures continue, changing only gradually over the decades, passing from one generation of Aggies to the next. Twenty years ago, when I was a student at Texas A & M, the most popular retaliatory measures were "drown-outs" and "Babbo bombs." My two older brothers had told me stories about these two measures long before my freshman year. In drown-outs, freshmen stalk unsuspecting sophomores while they are asleep—around 2:00 A.M. Since sophomores are not permitted to lock their doors while they are in the room, they are vulnerable to attack, but if they suspect something is afoot they can jerry-rig their closet doors so that intruders make a noise that will awaken them—hopefully.

Anyway, the freshmen involved fill trash cans with cold water, sneak into the sophomores' room, throw some fifteen to twenty gallons of cold water on the victims, and scramble back to their "holes," where they feign innocence and sleep. If the freshmen are not caught, the sophomores are left to clean up the mess, adding insult to injury. A member of the class of '63 told the following story:

> Our squad leader was a gung-ho, old army junior from Arlington, Virginia. He was really old army. We had a pretty sharp squad of freshmen—four of us. Every time one of us screwed up, we all got it. Our assistant squad leaders got into trouble, and the snowball got bigger as it rolled downhill. Anyway, they were always on our case. I think I did more push-ups for them than for all the rest of the sophomores put together. I guess they were pushing us to see how far we would let them take us. The second semester it got worse. Finally, we decided to drown their butts out! Early one morning we sneaked into their room—four of us with shitcans full of water. They were both sound sleepers—as a matter of fact, even though it was not their privilege, they had one of us come by each morning for a wake-up call. Anyway, on the count of three we threw our water on them and ran all over each other trying to get out of the room. We didn't make it. The skinny one, who slept on the top bunk, bounded out of bed at the same time the heavier one on the bottom bunk did, forking him across the neck with his legs. It was such a funny sight that we just stood there and laughed at them. They were pissed! We had to stay up the rest of the night cleaning up the room, but it was worth it. They told us later that they didn't think we had the guts to do it.

The Babbo bomb was an ingenious device which sometimes proved more potent and effective in retaliation than the drown-out. To make such a device, a freshman would purchase two large cans of "Babbo," a popular cleanser like Comet or Ajax. He would tap one can gently on the cement floor until the contents compacted into about half a can full. Then he would cut the top off the can, bore a small hole about halfway up the side of the can, place an M-80 firecracker into the can, with the fuse sticking out the hole, and begin pouring Babbo from the other can into his Babbo bomb, tapping it gently on the floor as he went. He could get about two whole cans into one. When the can was full, he put the top back on and taped it tightly. The Babbo bomb was ready for action.

The Babbo bomb, like the drown-out, worked best at night, when the victims were asleep. The freshmen sneak into the room, light the fuse, and roll the bomb across the floor. It has a very distinctive sound which, once heard, no one will ever forget: s-s-s thunk, s-s-s thunk, s-s-s thunk—kaboom! And voilà, the whole room is white, covered with fine gritty powder. It can take hours to clean up the mess.

Anyone who attended Texas A & M in the fifties could tell many stories about Babbo bombs. The following is a story I have heard repeated on more than one occasion, most recently during a visit with a former roommate of mine.

> We Babbo bombed ole L. and R. one night and got away. They lived a floor above us. They weren't our assistant squad leaders, but they gave us unmitigated hell; boy, how they loved to dump on us, and for no reason. We finally got tired of it and decided to Babbo bomb them. My ole lady [short for "fish ole lady," or freshman roommate] made the bomb, and we let them have it about three o'clock one morning. We jimmied their door so they couldn't get out and got clean away. They pretty well knew who did it, but had no proof. They kept giving us hell. We made a new bomb, only this time a dud, stole into their room after midnight one night, and rolled the ignited dud bomb across their floor. About the time the bomb should have gone off, we turned on their light to see what they were doing. They were both huddled in their bunks, scrunched into a corner against the wall with their blankets pulled over their heads. We laughed at them, which was harder on their egos than having to clean up their room again. They gave us trouble for a little while after that, but finally eased off.

I have heard countless stories about such experiences with Babbo bombs—most of them downright funny. One sophomore in our outfit whom we called Plato (behind his back, of course) tried to pull a John Wayne and throw the grenade back at the enemy; the bomb went off in his hand. He went around with his arm and hand in a sling for about a week, to the delight of all the freshmen.

While drown-outs and Babbo bombs were the two most popular retaliatory measures during the late 1950s and early 1960s, they were by no means the only ones. I've heard stories about freshmen burning cans of black shoe polish in an upperclassman's room, turning everything black; I've heard of floating upperclassmen's rooms—that is, stopping up the sink in the room and turning the water on, then plugging the crack under the door with a towel and letting three or four inches of water cover the floor (the University passed regulations against this practice while I was a student at Texas A & M, but it didn't stop it). I have heard of bombs made by drilling mud instead of Babbo; it's supposed to be far harder to clean up.

Another popular method of retaliation, at least in stories, involved the use of live or dead animals or poultry. Some of these retaliatory measures are striking enough to have been reported throughout the Corps. While I never knew of anyone who actually performed one of these acts, I have recently collected a number of stories by people who claim to have done so. One of the stories I heard some twenty years ago when I was a cadet is as follows:

> Two freshmen in the Vet Company found themselves being harassed unmercifully with little justification. Just before the Christmas break, the fish and their buddies planned revenge. After the upperclassmen left for home—early, of course—the freshmen went to one of the ag barns and "borrowed" ten live, healthy turkey gobblers, bought about three weeks' supply of feed for them, and brought them back to the dorm. They managed to get a passkey, and when the coast was clear, they entered the offending upperclassmen's room, placed the turkeys in the room with the feed supply, arranged the sink so that there would be a generous supply of water for the birds, and locked the door again. Anyone familiar with turkeys knows that they are great fertilizer machines, and they like to roost as high as they can. When the upperclassmen returned after Christmas break, their room was in shambles, filled with turkey droppings and feathers. They had to return the turkeys and clean up a thoroughly trashed room.

Another story concerns freshmen in the same company and involves a similarly imaginative turn of mind.

> During spring break [which lasts a week but which students manage to extend to ten to twelve days], a group of freshmen, angry at the treatment they had received at the hands of a couple of sophomores, got their revenge. They managed to get a passkey, and, using contacts in the vet school, managed to get a cow which had just died. Using a pickup, they managed to get it to the dorm and inside the upperclassmen's room. When the upperclassmen

returned a week or ten days later, they discovered a very ripe animal, swollen and oozing, which had to be dissected to be removed.

Neither of the above stories indicates the results of the retaliation measures, but they show considerable imagination and initiative.

This same theme, common in stories of twenty to thirty years ago, persists in stories told today. For example, the following account was recently collected from a junior at Texas A & M, who had heard it from a senior P. E. major from Squadron 9, class of 1976.

> Frank said that when he was a fish, there was a sophomore in another dorm that would hassle him and a fish buddy every time he saw them. After a month of unnecessary abuse, it was time to get revenge. Frank had been out one Saturday night, dancing, and on the way home, he picked up a dead skunk off the road and put it in a bag. He then went to his commanding officer and told him that his roommate had locked him out. The C. O. gave Frank the key that not only unlocked doors in Frank's dorm, but also the doors in the dorm where the annoying pisshead [sophomore] lived. It was about 12:30 a.m., and Frank took the passkey and the dead skunk quickly over to the sophomore's room. He first tried to see if the door was locked, and it was. He knew, then, that the sophomore was not there. He opened the door, took the skunk out of the bag, and crammed it into the air conditioner. He then turned the air conditioner and let it blow the rank fumes all over the room, left, and locked the door. Frank said that the sophomore never harassed him again.

While the structure and content of the stories told twenty years ago differ very little from those told today, certain elements are new, and new methods of getting even have blossomed in fertile minds and changing times. While skunks might have been placed in rooms twenty years ago, they were not placed in air conditioners because there were no air conditioners. Nor, as a matter of fact, are there today any hall and room floors to wax—a favorite pastime of freshmen of my day. Other changes in the dorms have provided other means of revenge, as the previous story indicated. When I was at Texas A & M, there were no phones in cadet rooms, just one public phone on each floor. A senior told the following story to one of my students in a folklore class:

> Chris told me of two pissheads who were roommates who had made all the freshmen do excessive push-ups and verbally abused them at every chance. The pissheads continually ragged on [harassed] all the freshmen for the slightest offenses. One evening the freshmen had a class meeting where they divided

up time blocks. Each fish received at least one fifteen-minute time slot. The freshmen called the sophomores on the phone at fifteen-minute intervals all night long, hanging up when they answered the phone. The sophomores could not take the phone off the hook because the university has a buzzer to prevent such action. The sophomores were kept awake all night long. They would sometimes do this on several nights in succession.

As I began making an inquiry into the subject at hand, I discovered a number of new terms for retaliatory measures, terms such as "white ratting," "quadding," and "sonic booming." The following is one Corps junior's description of "white ratting":

> White ratting is when you virtually turn a room upside down, pretending to be in search of a little white rat. You take out all of the dresser drawers and dump the clothes, flip the mattresses off the bunks and onto the floor, turn the desks on their sides. You remove the clothes from the closet and toss them into the room, knock the books off the bookshelf and pull the curtains down.

The definition of a Sonic Boom became clear in this story, told by a member of the class of '81:

> When I was a fish, I had a sophomore living next door who was constantly making me come by and was always picking on me, and I decided to give him a Sonic Boom. One night about 11:00, when I suspected the sophomore had gone to sleep, I put on my combat boots and walked over to the bunk. I grabbed the top bunk, jumped up and hurled myself flat-footed against the wall that joins my room with the sophomore's. This produced a very loud boom that not only startled the pisshead but also physically rocked him and his room. The books on the bookshelf fell to the floor, and everything that was not securely fastened to the wall also crashed to the floor. I quickly jumped into bed and tried to appear asleep when the sophomore came into the room. The pisshead was not fooled, and he gave me a come-by at 6:00 the next morning.

One of the most popular methods of taking revenge on sophomores is "quadding." [9] A "quad" is short for quadrangle, an open space between dorms. Unlike the Babbo bomb or drown-out, quadding calls for a different approach to "disciplining" the upperclassman and does not involve clandestine operations or attempted anonymity. The offending sophomore is summarily seized, stripped to his underwear, and hauled outside, where he is held helplessly pinned to the ground underneath a bathroom window. Other freshmen are waiting two or three stories up, with trash cans full of cold water, which they pour onto the helpless sophomore, often aimed at the crotch. The ploy works because of the safety-in-numbers principle. This sort of attack usually is reserved for sophomores who give problems to a large number of freshmen.

While the actual retaliatory measures change over time, their purpose remains constant.[10] As a matter of fact, the term "retaliatory measures" may miss the point. In a broader perspective, these measures—Babbo bombs, drown-outs, quadding, etc.—should be seen more as a process of restoring a sense of balance to the legitimate exercise of power and authority rather than as simply a matter of getting revenge. When there is abuse of authority, the freshmen take the socially sanctioned (though not institutionally approved) approach to dealing with the abuse of power. They do not "take revenge" on those they see as exercising legitimate authority in legitimate ways.

One other important aspect of the process must be noted. The use of these socially sanctioned retaliatory measures is assymetric; that is, one of a lower class may use these tactics against one of a higher class, but not vice versa. An upperclassman would never use these tactics on an underclassman. The power structure is such that there are institutional modes of exercising power downward, but extra-institutional methods must be used in the other direction.

The functions of the actual retaliatory acts are clear. They are pressure valves that permit potentially explosive, pent-up anger and frustration to be vented in a relatively harmless way. Pranks that are either hazardous or particularly costly are frowned upon. A social ideal is that vandalism should not be just to destroy; the idea is to cause physical discomfort and loss of time, a sort of repayment in kind. These episodes also serve to establish a strong sense of camaraderie among the initiates so engaged. The powerless seize power, even though for only a brief moment, even though the power must inevitably be relinquished. But how sweet it is when a Babbo bomb really works!

Now, one might ask, if these are the functions of the *acts* themselves, what functions do the stories about the acts serve? Clearly, they serve different functions for different groups. For the freshmen, they serve three broad functions. First, they teach freshmen the socially acceptable behavior for certain situations. It is not acceptable to get into a fist fight with an upperclassman or to attack him in other inappropriate ways; I have described some of the acceptable ways of dealing with an upperclassman who abuses his power. Second, the stories provide the freshmen with models for action in certain situations—this is how it is done! One doesn't have to be particularly inventive in discovering ways to get retribution; he just has to pay attention to tradition. And third, these stories provide vicarious release of frustration and anger, much the way trickster tales do in other societies.[11] Telling or hearing a good story about such an act of revenge is the next best thing to actually performing one, especially for the more timid.

For the upperclassmen and especially for those who have graduated and have moved on into other power structures, these stories provide a way of recalling and verbalizing experiences that lie at the heart of being an Aggie; one can recall the feelings that bind young men together in a way only the freshman Corps experiences can. At reunions, official and unofficial, these stories allow us to reestablish relationships with fellow Aggies, relationships that may have become tenuous over time. It is only appropriate that these stories be told in such Rites of Intensification as class reunions.

The freshman Corps experiences lie at the very heart of what it means to be an Aggie, at least for those who have gone through the Corps. Those outside the Corps will never—indeed, can never—feel the same way about the Aggie experience as one who has gone through the freshman experience in the Corps. Children have a meaning to mothers that they can never have for fathers, who did not carry them and who did not suffer the physical and emotional discomfort and pain in order to bring the children into the world. This is not to minimize the father's love or to say that it is somehow inferior. Nor would I argue that the spirit of Aggieland experienced and expressed by the civilian students is inferior or necessarily less—but it is different.

Nor, given the nine-month initiation that Corps freshmen go through, is there any wonder at the almost religious zeal and religious overtones of some Aggies' love for their school. Indeed, one finds similar initiations into many religious orders in both primitive and civilized societies.[12] Perhaps this is the reason there is more truth than poetry to this verse in the Aggie War Hymn (note that it is not called a fight song).

> You may boast of prowess bold,
> Of the school you think's so grand,
> But there's a Spirit that can ne'er be told.
> It's the Spirit of Aggieland.

Notes

1. The information for this paper is based upon my own experiences as a member of the Aggie Band from 1959 to 1962 and upon observations and reflections of members of

the Corps of Cadets, past and present. For four years I have served as advisor to B-Battery of the Aggie Band.

2. "High school hairy" is a pejorative label applied to the high school student (male) and especially to his "immature" behavior. The term clearly refers to the longer hairstyles of high school students, in contrast with the Corps haircut styles.

3. Arnold van Gennep, *The Rites of Passage* (Chicago: University of Chicago Press, 1960), 187.

4. Victor Turner, *The Ritual Process* (Chicago: Aldine Publishing Co., 1969), 94.

5. Ibid., 95.

6. "Dropping Handles" is a ritual in which a freshman and an upperclassman initiate a "first-name-basis" relationship, rather than the usual asymmetrical relationship. The upperclassman, who is in the position of power, initiates the ritual, except after Final Review when a freshman becomes a new sophomore, following which it is *his* responsibility to initiate the dropping of handles. In other cultures where there is a formal asymmetrical relationship reflected in the language—e.g., Spanish, Finnish, Latin, etc.—there are similar rituals initiated by the one in the superior position. In Finnish, for example, this is called a *sinunkauppa*, after which the participants call each other by first names and use the familiar form for "you," *sina*. *Sinutella* means to call one by his or her first name; *Teititella* means to call one by his or her last name.

7. Turner, *The Ritual Process*, 95.

8. Ibid.

9. "Quadding" has recently been outlawed by the University administration.

10. For example, the Babbo bomb was not known in the early 1940s, according to one informant who was a student at A & M then. It had become popular by the mid 1950s, when my oldest brother was a student at TAMU, and it disappeared sometime in the late 1960s or early 1970s. None of the Corps seniors of the Class of '80 knew what a Babbo bomb was.

11. Roger D. Abrahams, "Trickster, the Outrageous Hero," in Tristram P. Coffin, ed., *Our Living Traditions* (New York: Basic Books, 1968), 172; also, William A. Wilson, "The Paradox of Mormon Folklore," *Brigham Young University Studies* 17 (1976): 40-58.

12. Eliot Dismore Chapple and Carleton Stevens Coon, *Principles of Anthropology* (New York: Harry Holt and Co., 1942), 484-506; Turner, *The Ritual Process*, 1-43; Gennep, *The Rites of Passage*, 1-14.

(Photographs reproduced by permission of Don R. Swadley)

Please Drink the Water

SOME CURATIVE MINERAL WELLS OF TEXAS

by Don R. Swadley

Belief in the curative powers of highly mineralized water, taken internally or bathed in or both, has gone the way of the horse and buggy and hair oil. It takes some doing these days to enjoy—or suffer—a hot mineral water bath or to find mineral water, either whole or reconstituted from boiled-down crystals, that is certain to cure what ails you. Such was not the case as recent a time ago as my boyhood.

Texas radio listeners of the Thirties, especially those listening on WFAA, were bombarded daily with exhortations to take Crazy Water Crystals for their health. The crystals could be bought in any drug or grocery store, and people swore by them. I never used them myself but knew a number of people who did. The Dundee phone operator, an elderly widow who also took in boarders, claimed they kept her going, and she stirred herself up a glass every morning—regularly. Mineral water devotees who could afford to travel could pamper themselves in the luxury hotels and baths of such spas as Mineral Wells and Marlin. Those who couldn't afford the Baker and Crazy hotels of Mineral Wells or the Hilton of Marlin could settle for a boardinghouse, and even less affluent, or more individual, health-seekers could visit such comparatively obscure health centers as Wizard Wells in Jack County, Stovall Wells in Young, or Tioga in Grayson. Glen Rose in Somervell County and Arlington in Tarrant boasted wells the water of which tasted bad enough to convince people it had to be good for them.

Of the watering places cited only two still offer baths. Drinking the water as a cure has largely been replaced by tentative and wry-faced sipping by tourists, when such water can be obtained at all, and boxed crystals for reconsituting the water of the wells are sought after by antique buffs.

Among the spas of Texas, Mineral Wells was queen of them all. During the early years of this century a number of wells produced Mineral Wells' chief claim to fame, and hundreds of health-seekers flocked in, largely by rail, the year round. Bathhouses throve—all defunct now. You can no longer bathe at the Wagley, its former glory now fallen into deserted ruin, nor can you get the luxury hotel service, along with mineral water and hot baths, once available at the opulent Baker or Crazy hotels. The former is boarded up, and the latter is a retirement home. The smaller baths and boardinghouses that abounded have been converted for other uses, mostly housing apartments, and the pool in the terrace garden of the Baker is dried up and silent.

You can still get mineral water for drinking. The Famous Water Company— yes, that's its name—pipes water over West Mountain from its well to its downtown facility, where the water is bottled and sold in the surrounding area. Once you could have gotten it by the glass at the bar of the establishment.

With the spa business and Camp Wolters gone, downtown Mineral Wells is quieter than it used to be. You can't get a mule ride up the hills that surround the town, a favorite recreation of earlier days. You can, unlike the old days, get a beer, an ignominious end for a Texas water center, which now places its hopes for prosperity in industrial development.

The town of Marlin in Falls County is one of the two centers in Texas I know of where you can still get a commercially operated mineral water bath. The baths are linked managerially with the Falls Hotel, which was built by Conrad Hilton in 1930 as the eighth hotel in Hilton's famed career as "innkeeper to the nation." Hilton was betting on the continued popularity of the spa business, which had been important in Marlin since around the turn of the century; in this he made a mistake. The hotel closed in 1934 for a time, and Hilton sold it. Later reopened, the hotel still features Hilton's underground tunnel leading from the hotel to the bathing facilities across the street. The desk clerk allowed me to use the tunnel, saying that if I knocked at a door at the end of it, I would be admitted to the baths, which were not yet open for afternoon business. I heard voices which ceased when I knocked. After knocking awhile I tried the door, found it unlocked, and, not too sure of my welcome, entered what was obviously the lobby to the place. The two desk attendants preparing for afternoon business readily granted my request to inspect and take pictures of the facilities. These were in the process of renovation: tub replacement, new flooring, and other improvements. There was an exercise and therapy room with cleanly made-up beds where bathers could rest between baths. The tubs are in individual compartments and massages are available. I didn't take a bath, because they were $7.50, and it was only Friday. One of the charming desk girls offered to let me photograph her in the ladies' section—the sexes are of course segregated—but I declined through a combination of rectitude and of suspicion that she was putting me on.

The water at Marlin is more popular for external use than for internal health. A fountain next to the Chamber of Commerce building purports to supply the original Marlin Well water, the well being owned by the city, and of course I drank some. I could see why our forebears were certain it was curative, for they knew all good medicine tasted bad—and was even better for you if hot. Marlin water has both qualities. In the 1890s the state chemist supposedly certified the Marlin Well as "the deepest and hottest mineral well in the United States and richer in minerals than any other in the world." No one, except for members of my party, came near the fountain while I was around.

The fame and use of Marlin's baths and medicinal water have declined from the heady days of the past, but the baths and free drinking water are more than Mineral Wells can now boast. An informant states that she and a party spent a week in Marlin in 1945 solely because of Marlin's reputation as a spa. The only insect in the ointment was bedbugs, she said, but all in all she enjoyed herself. This was in wartime, when it was a treat to go anywhere voluntarily. John J. McGraw took the New York Giants to Marlin during training season from 1902 to 1932; who could argue with McGraw? It all had to be good for you.

During my boyhood I became keenly aware that Archer County natives had a reputation in the nearby metropolis of Wichita Falls as being a bunch of ignorant rustics. Larry McMurtry's *The Last Picture Show* has firmly established this canard nationwide. But WFAA's Jimmy Jeffries had told us all about Mineral Wells, although not many of us could go there, and a few of us knew about the Marlin water. On my side of the county—the north— nobody was aware that the adjoining county to the south featured mineral baths. Even novelist Benjamin Capps of Anarene, who bussed across the Archer county line to high school in Young County for a year before transferring to Archer City, says he had never heard of Stovall Wells as a boy. But it was there, near the town of South Bend, ten miles out of Graham, where the Clear Fork River joins the main Brazos. And now, as then, it is a mineral bath center for a small but devoted body of health-seekers. Soaking in its hot tubs will cure, or at least alleviate, all sorts of ailments, as a prominently displayed sign assures all who come to Stovall. Specified are rheumatism, athlete's foot, eczema, kidney troubles, ringworm, poison ivy, hay fever, soft gums, scalp diseases, sprains, bad colds, sores, stiff joints, poor circulation, hemorrhoids, cataracts, skin cancers, prostate troubles, psoriasis, earaches, arthritis, and infections. When I began my on-site visitations of mineral water centers in 1982 I still hadn't heard of Stovall Wells. Asking around that fall I found that one of my colleagues, who had grown up in Graham, had once "washed her feet" at some place nearby, and my neighbor of Shackelford County origin had heard of a place "somewhere up north of Breckenridge"—it might have been Ivan—that had a mineral bath of some kind. He remembered a story about somebody who threw a match into the bathing vat and caught its contents on fire, but that's all he knew.

I could have found the facts in Barbara Ledbetter's extensive research of Young County matters or in some such source, but I hadn't looked, and instead I lit out one morning for Ivan. It was a wide place in the road with two beer joints, the less dilapidated of which I entered to inquire about Stovall Wells. I thought I heard a rough-looking character in a "gimme" cap, who was loudly discoursing on coon trapping, interrupt himself to remark to his drinking companion, "Here comes 'Have Gun, Will Travel,' "—and not sotto voce. I wasn't up to playing the doughty Paladin and therefore ignored what after all I might just have thought I heard. The barmaid directed me some ten miles further to South Bend. Just as she had promised, out on the Clear Fork road, across the river in the flat valley, stood a cluster of white-and-silver-colored buildings.

The first thing you notice on approaching Stovall Wells is that you're in oil country. An otherwise fertile cultivated field to the east had a twenty-acre slush pit in it, and the oil smell was pervasive. I soon learned that all this had significance in Stovall's discovery. The 130 degree Fahrenheit water comes from what was intended in 1929 to be an oil well. A Dr. Stovall of Graham decided the water had medicinal value when bathed in—nobody would dream of drinking it—and began promoting the idea.

I don't have much information on the early history of the operation, which Dr. Stovall called Mystery Well. The promotional literature says that the curative property of the water was accidentally discovered by the children of an itinerant family who had "a peculiar skin disease." I suspect that the disease was the itch. Bathing in such water would indeed cure that. We had an outbreak of the itch in my town when I was in grade school, and my mother cured me with daily hot baths in strong carbolic acid and Lysol water along with applications of sulphur and grease. Stovall water contains all of these, and more.

Up close the Stovall buildings were less impressive than from across the river, where they shone in the noonday sun like the Taj Mahal. The wood and corrugated tin is neatly painted, however, and the grounds are clean— at least the front grounds. Behind the main building considerable disorder exists, characteristic of the oil field type: broken-down machinery, rusted pipes, oil-caked tanks. The great Clear Fork flood of several years ago, which washed out Albany and threatened the Hubbard Creek dam, also inundated the entire lower valley with floodwater that rose to nine feet in the main building of Stovall. Against that and other obstacles the present proprietor has made remarkable progress in his project to build up the place.

The lounge or lobby of the main building is cheerful and comfortable. Less "dressed-up" than the lobbies of the Falls or the Crazy, it struck me as a more pleasant place to sit than either of the others. There were tables for cards and other games suited to people who don't get around very well, and an elderly couple sitting out front was enjoying the simultaneous warmth of the sun and briskness of the north breeze. They had been coming from Plainview for twelve winters, they said, taking the baths and avoiding the high plains cold weather. And, they continued, the baths helped their rheumatism.

I took one of the baths, only $2.50 with a 25¢ towel fee. In the men's section were two eight-foot diameter pools. The water was about four feet deep, and there were graduated steps around the inside pool walls. Handrails enclosed the pools, and rope handholds dangled from above. One pool was hotter than the other; the three men present were bathing in this one when I entered. I chose the other pool. The water was black, from the large amount of petroleum in it. The three bathers were friendly and talkative, and they all praised the baths. One of them said he had cured a skin cancer by *two* twenty-one bath series (twenty-one being the number recommended by the management for best effects), and another said the bathing helped his arthritis. As I left a pitiful old man who had apparently suffered a stroke tottered into the bathing room. Stovall Wells has its believers. The proprietor has posted in a display case a large number of testimonials which, if weak in grammar and spelling, were strong in praise of what one of them called "this warters."

After about ten minutes of soaking—I could float without movement with my entire head clear in the buoyant water—I took a big drink of cold water and toweled off, feeling simultaneously exhilarated and rested. The literature advises leaving the minerals on the skin for at least twelve hours. I'm glad I didn't; my wife wouldn't have liked for her sheets to turn the black color the towel did. For all that night and the next day I carried the faint smell of petroleum around with me.

As Marlin and Stovall show, the hot bath cure has its followers even today. But it was much more so in our grandparents' time. Most people had to seek simple cures close to home, and watering centers, now inactive, supplied them with a way to do so. Tioga, for example, on which Jack Duncan is the chief authority now that his grandfather has passed on, still has one highly visible well, and there are plans for reviving Tioga mineral water and for rejuvenating the whole place. Jack tells about Tioga better than I can, so I will leave that to him.

Glen Rose on the Paluxy has a mineral water fountain on the courthouse square, but its main attraction these days is the dinosaur tracks and the restorative country living praised by John Graves. An informant, who in the early twenties used to go by foot and wagon from Cleburne to see the Glen Rose girls, tells me that he remembers Indian doctors practicing in Glen Rose who were definitely not members of the American Medical Association. The bathhouse of once-flourishing health center Wizard Wells near Jacksboro still stands waiting for the soakers and bibbers to return. Perhaps they will some day; I'd go there myself if there were a place to stay.

Even my adopted home of Arlington—which builds cars, tries to educate college kids, and furnishes living quarters for over one hundred thousand jobholders in what Dallas-Fort Worth boosters call the Metroplex—had a commercial mineral crystals operation during the Thirties. The promoter hoped to rival Crazy Water Crystals but failed. A downtown public well supplied mineral water that tasted so bad and had such strong internal effects that it played a part in the hazing process of North Texas Agricultural College freshmen. Every fall the students were marched downtown from NTAC and forced to drink copiously of the mineral well water—all for their health, of course.

Well, the old days are gone and with them the reign of water treatment. As I have tried to show, you can still lift a glass and soak your bones—but it just isn't popular anymore.

It All Wound Up in Bales

by Ernest B. Speck

The three traditional crops of southern agriculture were corn, cotton, and cane. Corn was consumed by man and beast, sorghum cane was fed to animals as hay and to people as sorghum molasses, but cotton was raised for money, although cotton seed was used as cow feed.

Because cotton is a hot weather plant, it was planted after corn and cane. The soil was prepared either by flat breaking or bedding, and a special plate was used in the planter to separate the seeds, which clung together because of the coating of fibers, and to drop them close together in the row. The sprouting cotton seeds had to be close together in order to assist each other in breaking the crust on the soil. But the close planting made for hard work later on. When the cotton was three or four inches tall, it had to be thinned out, and cotton chopping was a task requiring skill and fortitude. The proper tool for chopping cotton was a hoe with a blade some eight inches wide but no more than four inches tall. Depending on the fertility of the soil, the cotton chopper thinned down the cotton to one plant every ten to fourteen inches, deftly plucking out unwanted plants and leaving the others undisturbed. He also struck down any weeds that had begun to grow.

Discouraging weeds was an interminable task that went on all summer. In addition to the hoe, weeds were uprooted with the cultivator, which also broke the crust to preserve moisture. Cotton was hoed at least three times and plowed after each rain until the "squares" appeared. Squares are actually triangular in shape and are the bud out of which the bloom appears. It is on this square that the boll weevil is sitting in the "Boll Weevil Song," waiting for the boll to appear. The problem is that squares are easily knocked

129

off, and each lost square is a lost boll of cotton. Consequently, hoeing and cultivating could easily reduce the crop if not done with considerable care. One implement for cultivating that could be safely used at this juncture was the Georgia Stock. A one-horse plow, it had a wide sweep attached to its light wooden frame. A spindle-legged mule could pull the Georgia stock between the rows of cotton without touching a leaf. While we always longed for rain, we hoped there would be no driving thunderstorms with hail during the squares' tenuous lives.

The long summer was spent plowing the cotton when we were lucky enough to get rain. But one little ten-acre patch presented its own problem. This little strip of rich, sandy loam along Reed's Creek was often planted in cotton, but it was noted for always growing a bumper crop of bull nettles, a plant capable of putting man or horse in torment. A valiant creature such as old Roan would depart from decorous equine behavior in order to avoid contact with a bull nettle. Even a dead bull nettle can insert its tiny spines laden with poison into the hide of the unwary horse or human and cause intense discomfort.

The amount of hoeing needed to raise cotton in the days before tractors and Treflan, plus the heavy work of picking cotton, gave rise to the oft-repeated comment: "It takes two things to grow cotton, a strong back and a weak mind, and I ain't got either one."

While we scanned the sky every day, looking for a sign of rain, we knew that too much rain could be bad for cotton. The best weather is lots of sunny heat interspersed with showers that deposit enough moisture to be useful but that leave clear skies and sunshine behind. We called them cotton showers. Too much cloudiness is ideal for the growth of boll weevils.

If I may digress for a moment I want to tell a Mody Boatright story. I suspect it is not a solitary instance of an innocent child's making use of then forbidden language. The Boatrights had hired a family to do some hoeing for them. Little Mody observed that a young lady in the family was particularly skillful with her hoe. He commented to his mother that the girl was a good hoer. He was puzzled at his mother's negative reaction to his praise.

Finally, after all our summer labor in the cotton patch, late September and early October brought the cotton picking. The bolls popped open and the cotton fibers, with the seeds imbedded in them, began to hang in clumps. The boll opens in five sections, and each section of the hull culminates in a sharp point. To pluck out the cotton, the picker lowered his thumb and fingers so that each rested over a lock of cotton, then he pressed his fingers together and pulled out the cotton. But if he hit the points of the hull with his fingers very often he would be punished for his inaccuracy with sore fingers.

Picking cotton was perhaps the most arduous part of raising the crop. A good cotton picker could pick three or four hundred pounds in a day. But his hands had to be busy from daylight to dusk, and he spent most of the day walking on his knees dragging a heavy cotton sack. The cotton sack (homemade on all the small farms) was constructed of light canvas. It was about eight feet long, and it was a little over two feet wide. A strap, made of several layers of sacking stitched together, about three inches wide, was attached to the mouth of the sack and went over the shoulder of the picker. The last six feet or so of the sack had an extra layer of cloth, a kind of flap on the bottom, to keep the sack from wearing itself out as it was dragged along the ground. One corner of the bottom of the sack had a wad of seed cotton pinched off with a few strands of baling wire that were formed into a loop for hanging over the scales.

If a person picked five hundred pounds a day he could pick a bale in three days, but that could be done only in good cotton. A bale of cotton weighs roughly five hundred pounds, but it takes about fifteen hundred pounds of seed cotton to render a five-hundred-pound bale of fiber. We used to say that good cotton could "third itself," that is, yield one pound of fiber for each two pounds of seed.

There were assorted practices associated with picking and ginning cotton that were hardly typical of the piety our community liked to pretend it had. Since cotton pickers were paid by the pound, it was not unheard of for a picker to add a few rocks to his sack. The cotton was weighed on a steelyard type of scale hung from the tongue of a wagon elevated by being propped up by the doubletree. Since the owner of the cotton patch did not always watch the cotton being dumped into the wagon, it was easy to cheat with a few rocks.

A tale told by one of my kinsmen (probably about himself) concerned a young man who found a volunteer watermelon alongside a row he was picking. He thumped the melon and decided it could be ripe, but since it would have weighed about twenty pounds he was tempted to add the weight to his sack. But his conscience troubled him, so he cut the melon—it was just beginning to turn pink. He decided that it was a sign that honesty is not always the best policy, so he regularly put rocks into his sack from then on.

A most condemning story concerns the Methodist preacher who, like most parsons in the area, farmed to supplement the meager offerings his parishioners were able to provide. One device for adding weight to cotton was to wet it. Since cotton fibers readily absorb moisture, the weight can be increased considerably by the addition of water. The parson, wanting to give his income a healthy (if not holy) increase, poured so much water over his cotton that water dripped from his wagon. While those around snickered, the good parson sat on the spring seat of his wagon reading John Wesley as he waited for his turn at the gin.

Because cotton played such a large role in our lives it provided a few terms, some of which have modern variants. In addition to the cottontail rabbit, the cotton-headed child, the "Cotton-Eyed Joe," and the cottonmouth moccasin, there are the terms from the old grading system of the cotton-grading scale. *Middling* was, as the name suggests, in the middle. The top grade, oddly enough, was *Middling-fair*, even though *Fair* was the lowest grade. As has been noted, there are the "Boll Weevil Song" and cotton showers. And to be living in comfortable circumstances is to be *in high cotton*.

There are also the terms *cotton on to* and *cotton up to*, the latter less well known today. Carnivals sell cotton candy. To be *spitting cotton* is to be dry mouthed for lack of water. But most widespread is *cotton pickin'*, a term that is derisive and belittling, for cotton picking was looked upon as a task suitable only for the lowly. A modern variant is the CB term *cotton picker*, which is a euphemism used when SOB might otherwise be employed. And *boll weevil* can designate an ultra-conservative Democrat who supports Republicans.

The only medicinal use of cotton in our area that I know of was one employed surreptitiously. The juice from boiled green cotton bolls was believed to be an abortive. While green bolls were available only in the late summer, that was the time when the need was probably the greatest. Woods colts are most likely to be conceived, of course, when the warm breezes of spring start the sap, and other things, to rising.

Generally the seeds taken from the cotton were kept by the ginner in exchange for the ginning. This was a loss to the farmer; cotton seeds are a rich source of proteins and oils for cattle, and they have a nutlike odor and flavor. At the end of the harvest the farmer often wound up with some cotton that was not enough to make a bale. The ginner would usually buy the "remnant" and combine it with other remnants to make a bale, although a small amount was sometimes kept by the farmer for making quilts, cushions, and mattresses.

Before I turn to the raising of hay I want to describe an event that bit deeply into folk nature: when the government began to pay people not to produce. In the first year of the program, at the time farmers were being paid to plow up every third row, our cotton was about eight inches tall. Dad went into the field with a middle-buster to uproot the doomed plants. He turned at the end of each row and looked ruefully at the slain cotton, for it was only slightly short of murder for him to destroy plants he had nurtured up to that point.

Cane was still the principal sorghum grain raised for hay in our area in the thirties, although hegari (we called it "high gear") and maize were on the increase. We grew maize for its heavy heads, used for chicken feed, as well as for hay. We harvested the heads with a butcher knife and dropped them into tow sacks suspended from one shoulder by fodder twine.

Cane was ready to harvest in early summer when the heads began to harden and the lower leaves began to fade from green to pale yellow. It was mowed with a mower that could cut one row at a time. (It could cut a swath about two and half feet wide in broadcast crops, such as oats.)

After the cane had been cut and allowed to cure a day or two, it was raked into windrows and then into shocks with a rake some ten feet wide. A windrow is simply a row of hay extending across a field; it looks as if the wind might have blown the hay into such a pattern. The rake was then run along each windrow to gather the hay into piles, and it would trip itself when heavily loaded. Although we called them shocks, these little piles were not well-thatched shocks; they were soon dragged to the baler.

The system of moving the hay to the baler was rather primitive. A peeled willow pole eight to ten feet long was notched around the thicker end. In the notch were attached several strands of baling wire to which the clevis for a doubletree was affixed. The willow pole was run under a pile of hay, and the hay was fastened to the pole with rope. Two calf ropes were fastened at the notch on the pole and run over the hay at about thirty degrees above the ground on each side, attached to the pole with a couple of half-hitches. Or, instead, a single piece of rope was first secured at the notch on the pole, then run over the hay at thirty degrees from the ground, double looped over the other end of the pole, and then brought back over the other side of the hay to the notch at the front of the pole. The hay was then dragged to the baler.

The horse-powered baler consisted of a rectangular frame that shaped the bales, a plunger that pushed each forkful of hay into the frame, and a pole that connected to the plunger with an eccentric and drove the plunger as the outer end of the pole was pulled in a circle by a horse.

There were two very demanding tasks on a baler. The person who fed hay ahead of the plunger had to have a forkful of hay ready each time the eccentric tripped and the plunger returned to receive more hay. The other tough job was tying the bales. Wooden dividers were slipped into the baler every few minutes to separate the bales. Slots in the dividers provided space to insert the baling wires. Two wires were wrapped around each bale and "tied"; that is, the plain end of the wire was doubled back after being slipped through the loop at the other end and twisted around itself. The tyer had to keep the wooden dividers moving regularly through the baler, tie the bales as they moved along, take the finished bales as they emerged from the baler, and stack them or load them onto a wagon.

There were some difficulties in the hay harvest. We did not know the word allergy, but allergies were prevalent. Some people reacted to something in the hay; others had problems with the dust in the air. Whatever the basis for the reaction, many could not work with hay. The McCormick family did our baling, and one of the three sons could not work beyond noon before he would seek the shade of a nearby post oak and roll in misery while the baling continued. Another son, impervious to the tortures that afflicted his brother, would, with a native wizardry, keep the decrepit baler in operation. His father called him "mechanicy." The father could tie bales with amazing alacrity, despite a huge stomach, for two or three hours, when he would have to call on a third son to spell him. The fee for baling hay in the depression was a nickel a bale.

Of course we fed the baling crew on the day they were there, and they seemed delighted to have nothing more than plenty of corn bread, pinto beans, and sorghum molasses.

After the baling crew left, it was up to the farmer to get his hay under cover. We had a crib we used for hay that would hold quite a lot, so we usually had only the chore of hauling the hay from the field to the barn. On the few occasions when we had more hay than could be stored in the barn, we stacked it nearby and covered it with a tarp. The tarp was one Dad had used when he travelled in a covered wagon from Baird (near Abilene) to Llano County dragging a cultivator behind him. That journey, late in 1930, might be one of the last covered wagon migrations in Texas. At any rate, his wagon sheet became our cover for hay and fodder stacks.

Hay has also made its contributions to our vocabulary. One *hit the hay*, whether the hay was in a tick or not, and a *quick roll in the hay* also made use of hay's resiliant characteristics. Other terms include *hayseed, hay head, haymaker, haywire, hayburner, needle in a haystack, make hay while the sun shines,* and *that's not hay.* But the item—and term—the hay-harvesting process contributed that became a major feature of American rural life was baling wire. A *baling wire job* is a piece of work easily fixed with baling wire or one done in a slipshod fashion. Everyone knew that nothing ever went wrong with a Model T Ford that baling wire could not correct.

Some measure of the value of the two crops and the labor that went into them can be seen in the payment a sharecropper paid to the landowner in order to grow these two crops. A cropper who furnished his own seed and team would pay the owner one-third of the hay (or corn) for the use of the land, but he had to pay only one-fourth of the yield of his cotton. The one cropper we had generally grew enough corn and hay to feed his two scrawny mules and enough cotton to buy himself a supply of Brown's Mule chewing tobacco. He could not have wished for more.

LINDA M. FELTNER

Coyote

THE SUFFERING SAVIOR

by Blake Burleson

here is a figure in the mythology of the Indians of the American Southwest that stands paramount over all others. This leading figure of the myth age is thought to be the oldest personage of these ancient traditions. His generic cousins in cultures worldwide are also considered by many to be the oldest in their lore. Yet this psychological gem is no hero. He is no Zeus, no pious Aeneas, no King Arthur, no Lone Ranger. He is not held in awe. He is not worshipped. He is not even respected. Instead, he is laughed at, ridiculed, degraded, and looked down on. His name is Coyote.

Many today have been unknowingly introduced to the Coyote of Indian folklore through the Saturday morning television cartoon entitled "The Road Runner Show." This cartoon borrows its primary character, Wiley Coyote, from the Indian mythological figure. The cartoon portrays, even if tediously, the basic Coyote tale. Wiley Coyote tries endlessly to capture the speedy roadrunner but never succeeds. His best-laid plans to trick the prey always backfire, and he is the one, in the end, who is tricked. Yet Wiley Coyote never learns from his mistakes; he never gives up the ridiculous quest. And he always suffers.

This type of personage, displayed by Coyote, is known as the Trickster. Carl Jung recognized the Trickster as a universal archetype that could be evidenced in societies around the globe. For instance, the Trickster of the European is Reynard the Fox; the Trickster of the southern Negro is Br'er Rabbit; the Trickster of the African is often the hyena or jackal. The list could go on.

137

In North America the principal Trickster figures of the Indians, in addition to the Coyote, include the Raven, the Mink, the Rabbit, and the Bluejay. Among the Indians of the Southwest, and especially among the nonagricultural tribes in this region, it is the Coyote who reigns as chief Trickster. In Texas, the Coyote can be found among the Caddo, the Lipan-Apache, the Kiowa, the Kiowa-Apache, the Comanche, and the Wichita.

All of these Trickster types are defined by Jung as collective "shadow" figures. By that he meant that the Trickster represented all that was inferior to a culture and corresponded to a psyche that had hardly left the level of an animal.[1] He interpreted the Trickster as

> a primitive "cosmic" being of divine-animal nature, on the one hand superior to man because of his superhuman qualities, and on the other hand inferior to him because of his unreason and unconsciousness.[2]

The Coyote of the Indians, like all Tricksters, is characterized by this "shadow" nature; he is a buffoon, a negator, and a destroyer. Yet it would be wrong simply to equate the Coyote with evil. The Coyote has a positive function as well. There is an aura of the sacred surrounding the Coyote. This attitude can be seen in the numerous names given to him. He is called God's Dog, Father Coyote, First Born, The Medicine Dog, Voice of the Night, Old Man Coyote, First Creator, Chief Coyote, The Great Spirit's First Lieutenant, Old One, Gray Dusk, and The Ancient.

What then can we make of this sacred buffoon? Is he a god? J. Frank Dobie writes that "to many tribes within its range, the coyote stood—yet stands totteringly—as a god. . . ."[3] Yet the Coyote was never worshipped as a deity. Perhaps the highest title that can be bestowed on him is that of savior. Mac Linscott Ricketts devotes a portion of his six-hundred-page dissertation on the Trickster to this idea.[4] The remainder of this paper is an exploration of the savior concept as applied to Coyote. Two questions are asked. First, how is Coyote a savior? And second, what does this kind of savior reveal theologically?

In answering the first question, that is, how does Coyote save, a specific Indian myth is examined. The myth is concerned with the origin of death, a tale found throughout most tribal groups in North America. In nearly all of these tales, the Trickster is portrayed as the marplot who is responsible for bringing death into the world. The basic plot of the story is presented here.

> In the beginning of the world, when the animal people were created, when trees and grass and animals and birds were people, everything was going along

well. It went along until the middle of time. There was no death. They began to talk about it. Some said it would be best to have death. Others were against it. They talked about it. Many wanted to live forever. Coyote was the one who said, "I want death to exist."

The others said, "Well, if there must be death, let them die and we will put them away, but let them come back to life in four days."

"No," said Coyote, "I'll take this pebble and drop it in the water. If it floats there will be no death, but if it stays down, then there will be death. They will not come back to life in four days."

So Coyote dropped that stone in the water. It never rose to the surface. The Coyote said, "Well, you see that. When people die they cannot come back to life any more."

Coyote was the very first to lose a child. He said, "You people said that when anyone died he would come back in four days."

The others answered, "No, you are the one who talked against it. You were the one who threw the stone in the water so that the dead would not come back."

Then the Coyote started to cry. He put his child away. After that people died.[5]

It would appear to me that this myth more than any other displays the saving, that is, the redemptive, aspect of Coyote. Although Coyote is responsible for death, it is the same Coyote who is the agent of redemption through death. The death of his son secures Coyote's place as a suffering savior.

There are two reasons why Coyote is able to redeem the situation through his suffering. The first, as indicated by Ricketts, is the laughter that this tale brought. The sheer absurdity of the situation, that of ordaining death and then being the first to suffer its pain, was indeed hilarious to the Indian. Anyone who has lived among primitive peoples knows of their uncanny instinct for laughing at suffering. Certainly this is a saving grace—the ability to laugh at life's ambiguity. Ricketts writes that Coyote "endures their ridicule . . . and in the end saves them, through their laughter." [6]

The second explanation is perhaps more fundamental than the first, although it is related to it. Not only does Coyote suffer the loss of his son, he also suffers the degradation of being tricked at his own game. This "Guiler Beguiled" concept contains an important aspect of redemption which can be seen in other traditions.

I am suggesting that there is, in fact, a significant parallel between the Indian story above and the patristic doctrine of atonement found in the medieval church. This "classic" Christian theory of salvation apparently fulfills the same need for the medieval Christian as the death-of-the-Coyote's-son story does for the Indian.

The shared elements of the Indian story and the biblical story are easily located. First, man is tricked into death. The Indian is tricked by the Coyote; Adam by the Serpent. Second, redemption is brought about through death. The Coyote suffers the death of his son; God suffers the death of his son. The question to be asked at this point is: What apparent need of man is being met by both of these stories?

The church fathers, beginning with the patristic era, sought to work out theologically exactly how the death of Christ met man's redemptive need. The patristic theory (also called the Abuse-of-Power, the "classic," or the *Christus Victor*) has been disdained by modern theologians for the same reason that the medieval mind held it in respect. Namely, it is derived from the folklore figure of the Trickster himself. Kathleen Ashley has pointed this out in her study of Christ and Satan as theological Tricksters in medieval religious literature.[7]

The patristic theory of atonement explicitly describes the Incarnation as a divine trick to entrap the Devil. According to this theory, when the Devil tricked men into sin he won the right to take them into death. In order to redeem man, Christ disguised himself in human form and tricked the Devil into killing him. This was an abuse of the Devil's legitimate power since Christ was sinless. Henceforth, the Devil's claim to men's souls is cancelled. Greek and Latin fathers—including Irenaeus, Origen, Athanasius, Basil the Great, Gregory of Nyssa, Gregory of Nazianzus, Cyril of Alexandria, Cyril of Jerusalem, Ambrose, Augustine, and Gregory the Great—all adopt this theory.[8] Augustine even speaks of the "mousetrap" in which the bait is Christ's flesh, enticing the Devil into the trap of the Divine Trickster.[9]

This theory, in which the Devil is outwitted at his own game, interprets redemption in the same manner that the Coyote story does. Both, and here is the common element, *satisfy the folk instinct for justice*. The Coyote, who tricked the Indian into death, becomes the victim of his own game, just as the Devil, who deceived mankind, is outdone by Christ through deception. The Guiler, in both cases, is Beguiled. This knowledge—that justice has been done, that the Trickster has been tricked—better enables the common man, whether he be American Indian or medieval European, to endure his suffering.

This same folk instinct for justice is still with us today. Stories depicting one who succeeds by means of trickery and then loses all through another one's trick are commonplace at the cinema. The recent box office hits "Raiders of the Lost Ark" and "Trading Places" are excellent examples of this theme.

While Coyote as suffering savior has the same redemptive role that Christ does in the medieval church, there are also some great differences. In fact, Coyote is significantly different from most savior figures found in the major world religions. Coyote lacks a basic element characteristic of most divine or semidivine redeemers: the Coyote does not save man from the space-time world, from the here and now. He is unlike the Christ of Christianity, the "Soshyan" of Zoroastrianism, the "Son of Man" of Judaism, the "Mahdi" of Islam, "Maitreya" of Buddhism, and "Kalkin" of Hinduism, all of whom deliver mankind from the evil of the present period into the bliss of a new age.

This element of salvation from the here and now is seen not only in the major world religions but also among primitive groups. Mircea Eliade has suggested that messianic movements in primitive cultures invariably involve a "quest" for paradise or utopia.[10] Salvation is seen as deliverance from the space-time world. Generally speaking, it would seem that the savior figures of the world redeem man from his historical situation.

Coyote, the suffering savior of the Indians, does not, however, save man from his predicament. It is in this sense that he is an *inverted savior*. The only redemption that he effects is in the here and now, not in the hereafter, not apart from the mundane world. What does this kind of savior reveal, then, theologically?

Ricketts, in his study of the Trickster, has pointed to the religious significance of this mythological figure.[11] Ricketts basic premise is that the Trickster, and for our study the Coyote, is an "irreligious" or antireligious personage in the traditional sense. Unlike the shaman or priest who tries to appease the supernatural and cooperate with it, the Trickster confronts the supernatural and tries to overcome it. The basic mind-set of the Trickster holds that life can be fully lived without being supported by supernatural grace. It is, as Ricketts says, a "worldly religion."[12]

The Trickster does not save man from the space-time world because, for the Trickster, this is all there is. According to Ricketts the Trickster is man being fulfilled through humanism—that is, without God. "He is man, muddling through some of life's problems, discovering his own powers of mind and body, and using them, sometimes wisely, sometimes foolishly."[13] Thus, it is not the transcendent world, but this world, the here and now, that is sacred. His way is a way of secularity, a way of profanity. He "demythologizes" the fears and the wonders of the supernatural world. The salvation or redemption that he brings through the death of his son is not one of a future hope. It is, instead, a "realized eschatology." Death is final and death brings suffering. Yet death is to be accepted, and instead of straining to circumvent one's mortality through religion, one should simply live. This is the message of the Coyote. His is a religionless faith in life.

This theology or philosophy was apparently that of J. Frank Dobie (who was one of the editors of the Texas Folklore publication in 1938, *Coyote Wisdom*). The epitaph that Dobie wrote for himself reads:

> He loved life and put a few fragments of it into writing. Because of deference to the well-mannered he failed to expose most of what he knew, enjoyed and hated. He achieved a liberated mind. Realizing that all gods and bibles are man-made, he had contempt for all creeds, and admiration for nobilities and sensible skepticisms. His faith in the geological processes of the universe, including the speck called Earth, was, like literature, a solace to him.[14]

Certainly this is the wisdom of the Coyote speaking through Dobie.

In addition, the same kind of religionless faith or worldly religion that the Coyote proclaimed has taken form in Christian circles in this century. Dietrich Bonhoeffer, the great German theologian who was executed by the Nazis in 1945, is often credited with beginning a movement in Christianity that has been called Radical Theology. Several points of affinity with Coyote theology can be noted. Bonhoeffer believed that the church should stand against religion. Religion, to him, was a selfish attempt at self-preservation. He instead advocated a "religionless Christianity." This kind of Christianity called for an affirmation of life in the space-time world. The Christian should be world-affirming and should live as a man among men. This existence in the world should be characterized by *hillaritas*. It should be a laughing religion. It should be a way of life in which man relies on himself and not on a deus ex machina.

Bonhoeffer's influence can be seen in the work of other Christian writers such as John A. T. Robinson. In his book, *Honest to God* (which sold more copies in its first year after publication than any other publication in theology in the history of the world,[15] Robinson writes of a "worldly holiness" or a "holy in the common."[16] This same "religionless," life-affirming attitude can be seen in men like Harvey Cox (*The Secular City*), Martin van Buren (*The Secular Meaning of the Gospel*), and Jürgen Moltmann (*The Passion for Life*).

What, then, in conclusion can we say about the Coyote of the Indians? The Coyote is a suffering savior. He redeems man by virtue of his ability to make the Indian laugh. Laughter amidst the ambiguities of life is purging. And he redeems because he satisfies a longing in man for justice. Yet Coyote is an inverted savior. He does not save man from his predicament. Instead he gives man the incentive to live the life that he has here and now.

What I have tried to do is to explore the meaning of the Trickster theology by drawing parallels from the Christian tradition. These apparent similarities between an animistic and a monotheistic religion suggest that the primitive man is a not-so-distant cousin to us. These affinities also point to the universal and persistent attraction of the Trickster. The call of the Coyote still echoes inside of us. "If we laugh at him, he grins at us. What happens to him happens to us." [17]

Notes

1. Carl Jung, *Four Archetypes*, trans. by R. F. C. Hull (Princeton: Princeton University Press, 1959), 150.
2. Ibid., 144.
3. J. Frank Dobie, *The Voice of the Coyote* (Boston: Little, Brown, and Co., 1949), 265.
4. Mac Linscott Ricketts, "The Structure and Religious Significance of the Trickster-Transformer-Culture Hero in the Mythology of North American Indians" (Ph.D. diss., University of Chicago, 1978), 1.
5. The form of this tale can be seen among numerous tribes. See the Maidu tale in J. Frank Dobie, Mody C. Boatright, and Harry H. Ransom, eds., *Coyote Wisdom* (Austin: Texas Folk-Lore Society, 1938), 68; the Lipan-Apache tale in Morris E. Opler, *Myths and Legends of the Lipan Apache Indians* (New York: American Folklore Society, 1940), 38-39; and the Caddo tale in George A. Dorsey, *The Traditions of the Caddo* (Washington: Carnegie Institute of Washington, 1905), 15-16.
6. Ricketts, 605-6.
7. Kathleen M. Ashley, "The Guiler Beguiled: Christ and Satan as Theological Tricksters in Medieval Religious Literature," *Criticism: A Quarterly for Literature and the Arts* 24 (1982): 126-37.
8. Gustaf Aulén, *Christus Victor: An Historical Study of the Three Main Types of the Idea of Atonement*, trans. by A. G. Herbert (New York: Macmillan Co., 1961), 37-39.
9. Hastings Rashdall, *The Idea of Atonement in Christian Theology* (London: Macmillan, 1925), 364.
10. Mircea Eliade, *The Quest* (Chicago: University of Chicago Press, 1969), 88-111.
11. Ricketts, 600-608.
12. Ibid., 602.

13. Ibid., 604.
14. Lon Tinkle, *An American Original: The Life of J. Frank Dobie* (Boston: Little, Brown, and Company, 1978), 249.
15. David L. Edwards, ed., *The Honest to God Debate* (Philadelphia: Westminster Press, 1963), 7.
16. John A. T. Robinson, *Honest to God* (Philadelphia: Westminster Press, 1963), 84.
17. Paul Radin, *The Trickster* (New York: Philosophical Library, 1956), 169.

Illustration, Coyote, *by Linda M. Feltner.*

A Texas Planked Pirogue

THE CADDO LAKE BATEAU

by James Conrad and Thad Sitton

A mong Texas folk craftsmen, Wyatt A. Moore of Karnack is something of an anomaly; he builds traditional wooden boats. Although his business card identifies him as "Riverboat Pilot" and "Consultant," and although he has held just about every job possible from roughneck to fishing guide to whiskey cook, Moore, eighty-four years old, is now perhaps best known as the last surviving builder of Caddo Lake bateaus.

Moore has built many bateaus and paddle skiffs in his lifetime. Other boat-builders in the Caddo Lake area—the most famous being the legendary Frank Galbraith, Wyatt Moore's mentor—made bateaus from the turn of the century into the early 1950s, but these boatmen are no longer alive.

The bateau—a flat-bottomed, one-person, canoelike craft with a live-box and minnow well partitioned off amidships—was once indispensible around swamplike Caddo Lake and was the basic component of the fishing, hunting, and moonshining equipage of many natives. Its narrow, flat bottom enabled the bateau to snake through the cypress "islands" and slide over the endless meadows of lily pads which make the Texas end of Caddo something of an aquatic maze. Paddling was all but effortless, and cargo room was ample. The boat was much favored by moonshiners because it gave them access to cypress islands in the lake—shallow, heavily timbered areas where illegal distilleries could be mounted on carefully hidden plank platforms. When operations got too risky in one location, bateaus could be used to transfer the still to another platform in another part of the lake. A revenuer or other lawman was not going to use a bateau, and nothing else could penetrate the swamp. During the years that Moore made whiskey, he had bateaus that

145

occasionally transported up to eight hundred pounds of mash.

Even as late as the 1950s, after the introduction of motors and of aluminum and fiberglass boats, fishermen and hunters still used bateaus, but they would tie them to the back of their motorboats and tow them to the fishing or hunting grounds. They would then anchor the motorboats and use the bateaus to hunt or fish.

Moore's bateau (the name is simply the French term for boat) seems to be a Texas variant of the Louisiana planked pirogue described by William Knipmeyer in his classic study "Folk Boats of Eastern French Louisiana."[1] Acadian planked pirogues evolved from French dugout pirogues, which in turn had evolved from Indian dugouts. The planked version developed sometime in the last decades of the nineteenth century, in association with the spread of large-scale cypress lumbering operations. The cypress plank pirogue at Caddo Lake, however, seems to have developed special features to meet special circumstances. First, it was often larger than the typical Louisiana pirogue—around sixteen feet instead of fourteen feet. Caddo Lake combines a wooded swamp on the Texas side with large stretches of exposed open water in Louisiana, so the larger size of the boat, along with the flat, rockered[2] bottom and the low center of gravity (the bateau paddler sits on the bottom to ensure stability), may represent something of a "big water" adaptation. The flat, rockered bottom and flared sides[3] also work well for threading the mazelike cypress islands on the Texas side and for sliding over the water vegetation—characteristics that can be fully appreciated only by someone who has actually tried to navigate in the frustrating world of the swamp.

Another special feature of the Caddo bateau was its built-in fishwell and live-box. The Texas pirogue was often specialized for fishing, incorporating a lattice-covered fish box that could be flooded by pulling out plugs in the sides of this special chamber. To balance the water-laden live-box, the bateau's paddler sat forward of the midline of the boat. When no water was in the fish box, the fisherman compensated for the bateau's bow-heavy configuration by carrying ballast in the stern—a most unusual arrangement for a sixteen-foot boat! In addition, a skeg (fixed directional rudder) was mounted below the stern to give directional stability and to help the rocker-bottomed craft track straight.

Although the bateau's day is past, it stands as a testament to the resourcefulness and craftsmanship of Wyatt A. Moore and of other early boatbuilders who learned well the lessons of Caddo Lake. Moore and his bateau are still capable of venturing where few others can go. As he says, "The old-time fishing boat was a tool of the trade, and was designed to fit that purpose." As an ingenious folk technology for exploring the watery resources of the Caddo Lake swamplands, Moore's bateau works as well as it ever did.

Wyatt Moore is retired, but he was persuaded in the spring of 1983 to build one last bateau so that the details of the construction of this traditional Texas folk boat might be fully recorded on film and videotape. On June 28, 1983, Moore, with the skilled assistance of carpenter Paul Ray Martin of Uncertain, Texas, began work on the bateau. By late that afternoon the boat was completed, except for some minor finishing work, sanding, and painting. The next day, after a special treatment to temporarily seal and waterproof the craft, the builders launched and successfully tested it on the waters of Caddo Lake. In its heyday, back in the 1920s and 30s, such a boat would have sold for around thirty-five dollars. Modern reproduction costs for the bateau are about one hundred dollars, excluding labor.

As a result of the boatbuilding experiment, a special traveling exhibit on the "Last Caddo Bateau" was prepared by the Oral History Program of East Texas State University. This exhibit, which features the boat itself, as well as a collection of black-and-white photos of the boatbuilding process, was made possible by a grant from the Texas Committee for the Humanities of the National Endowment for the Humanities. The Texas Folklore Society acted as the official sponsor of the grant application.

The plans, line drawings, and comments by boatbuilder Wyatt Moore included below all relate to the "last Caddo bateau" constructed by Moore and Martin in 1983. For a more detailed description of the boat construction process as well as an extensive life history of Moore, see *Every Sun That Rises: Wyatt Moore of Caddo Lake* (Austin: University of Texas Press, 1985).

WYATT MOORE ON THE CADDO LAKE BATEAU

All my life I've fiddled with boats. I 'spect I've built 180 to 200, all wood boats. I like wood. A wood boat is much better for one's health than a metal one. The vibrations of a metal boat have a very adverse effect on a person's central nervous system—causes headaches and high blood pressure. Mother lived to be over ninety years old, and she rode only in wood boats. A wood boat absorbs vibration and soothes one's nerves. Why, an outboard will last two or three times longer on a wood boat than a metal one. In hot weather,

Wyatt Moore builds a Caddo Lake Bateau

the shade under a wood boat is cool. A metal boat is hot and drives away fish. Besides, if a metal boat fills with water, it sinks. A wood boat floats.

But boatbuilding is not like piling up some brush. If you don't do it right you wind up with something crooked.

Once, nearly everybody felt that one of those little fishing boats was a necessity, not a luxury. You couldn't go out there and do a hard day's fishing in a big old hard-to-paddle boat and get up in here, there, and yonder and cover lots of territory and keep the fish alive. The old-time fishing boat was a tool of the trade and was designed to serve that purpose.

I used to use one of 'em a good deal in the fall of the year. I would take a Buelspinner on a cane pole and troll the edge of the timber and hunt the squirrels out over the water and fish in combination with it and/or maybe kill a duck. I'd come in with ducks, squirrels, and a few fish, everyday. I hauled a full-grown deer from up the creek in one, one day. And during the seven or eight years I almost exclusively made whiskey, I had a bateau I had carried eight hundred pounds of whiskey in. I knew they couldn't out-paddle me in a bateau boat, and I could go places where they couldn't go. Here, our method was mostly to put a platform out over the water in Caddo Lake in thickets where only a small canoelike boat could get into and run five or six barrels of mash. I never did plow one of Jim Ferguson's mules, but some of my friends told me that they thought I would finally make it, but I didn't quite.

The bateau was twelve feet long, I believe, pointed at both ends and decked in. I built so many that I cannot keep up with them. I built two or three fourteen-foot, little butt-ended ones and decked them in and put a wave board along the sides, up and down and around. They are gone. My brother took one to Fort Worth and I think lost it up there or sold or traded it off or something. I get to thinking back about some of those boats I built and I wish I had kept them, I guess, since I've gotten too old to build another one. But unless you used it, I don't guess you'd need it.

People coming in for me to build them one could look at another boat and say, "Well, I'd like mine a little wider or a little this or a little that." Then I could pub a bevel square in there and take a pattern off it and go ahead and make slight alterations on it. If a fellow wanted a boat I'd get hold of my blueprints and sort of build it to whatever purpose he wanted it. But if I wanted to slightly change it, I would. I'd have the board hanging up in the shop. Maybe I would use that board later to make a boat of it.

I never knew of anybody getting drowned in one of the things. They respected 'em more, I guess. Down on the Big Lake, at James' Bayou, which comes in from the north, it's about a mile wide. The north wind sweeps down through there, and I have heard somebody way back yonder talking about some fellow come across there in one of 'em one day, and part of the time you couldn't see him, 'cause the waves was so high. Course, one man in an empty boat, he'd probably set down low in the bottom, and it'd withstand a lot of waves.

Now there was a man, Eddie McCathrin, who couldn't swim a lick, used one of 'em all his life 'till he was old. He finally died on one Christmas day from overdrinking corn whiskey, but he never did drown in a bateau! And he had a uncle couldn't swim, and he used one. He said if he turned over, he'd go to the bottom and walk to the bank. But he couldn't have and never did. And when he went to the river he'd go along the edge, and I've seen him drunk in his boat—he'd stick to the bank. And I never heard of but one man drown in 'em. He was a city dude whose financial difficulties overwhelmed him and he went off down the Lake in one and was found drowned and the boat floating. He sunk, but the boat didn't.

THE BATEAU CONSTRUCTION

Shaping the Mulberry Stems
The first step in the construction of the boat is the preparation of the mulberry stems for the bow and stern pieces. Moore quarters a mulberry log with an axe and sledgehammer; then a precise, almost imperceptible, taper is cut, with the narrow end at the bottom, to give the exact pitch needed to prevent the plank sides from cramping at the end.[4] (Two smaller, wedge-

shaped pieces of mulberry must be cut to serve as stem guards, but these are added only after construction is nearly completed, when the decking is done.)

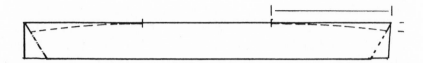

Cutting the Side Boards

Two 16' x 1' x 5/8" Louisiana red cypress planks form the sides of the boat. Moore cuts the ends of these boards to form identical bow and stern angles. He then proceeds to scribe shallow angles along the top of the front one-third of each end of each board—angles that are deepest at the ends and shallowest about 5'4" toward the centers of the boards. These wedge-shaped slices are trimmed off both ends to keep the sides of the boat from sticking up too high in proportion to the bottom. Depending on the shape of the boards, Moore sometimes takes a strip (semicircle in shape) from the bottom at midpoint along the edge of the board. After cutting the same end angles from the second board and trimming off the upper edges, he carefully uses a hand plane and drawknife to make them exactly alike.

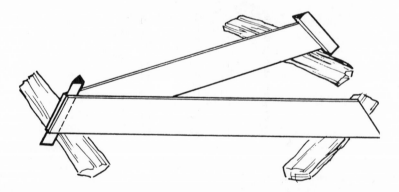

Nailing the Side Boards to the Bow and Stern Stems

The two ends of one of the side boards are nailed to the bow and stern stems with about 3" sticking out above and below the board. (The bow and stern stems are the same shape and size.) The second side board is placed and nailed against the front bow stem. According to Moore, it is crucial that the two boards are at the same height on the stem.[5]

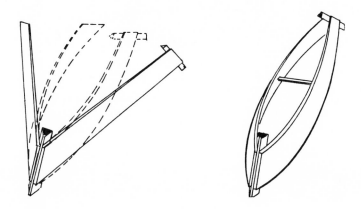

Bending the Side Boards Together

After nailing the two sides to the bow stem and one side to the stern stem, Moore inserts a temporary divider (slightly wider than the bulkhead) between the two side boards and then cautiously brings the two open side boards together and nails them at the stern stem.

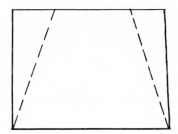

Cutting the First Bulkhead

Three bulkheads, the first placed 7'5" from the bow, the second 6" from the first bulkhead, and the third 3'3" from the second, serve to create a minnow well and a live-box for fish, as well as to give the boat its width and profile. The first bulkhead measures 33" at the widest end (top) and 20" at the narrow end (bottom). Moore saws this bulkhead but waits to custom fit the others after the first bulkhead has been nailed into place.

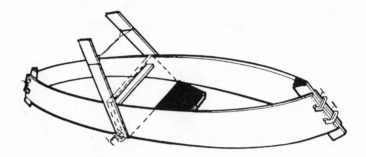

Bending the First Bulkhead in Place

After nailing the two ends to the stern stem, Moore builds a viselike rig of two 4' strips of lumber anchored with c-clamps to the side boards. The bending boards are then gradually brought together, twisting the side boards around the first bulkhead. Finally, nails are driven into the sides to secure the bulkhead in place.

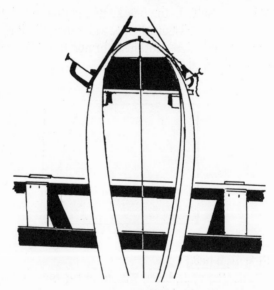

Checking the Alignment

At this point, Moore checks the alignment by placing the boat perfectly level on sawhorses and stretching a string right down the center of the boat from stem to stern. The sides on the right and left of the string should seem perfectly equal. Next, Moore inserts the second and third bulkheads to fit the curve and shape of the side board. The rule of thumb is to work to the angle that has the most flair.

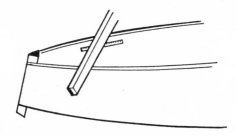

Placement of Cross Supports

With the bulkheads as spacing guides, ribs or knees about 3" x 2" are inserted about every fifteen inches to give additional support and bracing to the craft.[6] Again, like the bulkheads, Moore uses the side with the most pitch for the angle of both sides of the side.

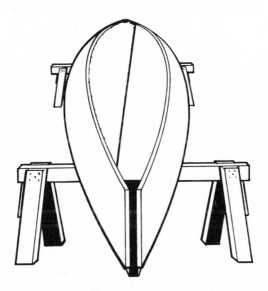

Fitting the Bottom

As a necessary preparation for the next step—nailing the bottom—Moore planes the bottom of the ribs, bulkheads, and side boards level and flat.[7]

The bottom boards (also made from 16' x 1' x 5/8" cypress planks)[8] are cut at a slight angle to the center, thus allowing the end seams to remain in the water when the boat is beached to keep them swollen shut. Moore and other traditional bateau boatbuilders do not use any kind of caulking for their craft; instead, lead base paint (usually green) is applied to the bottom boards, ribs, and sides. While the painted boards are still wet, he places furniture clamps at both ends and in the middle to squeeze the bottom tightly in place before nailing.

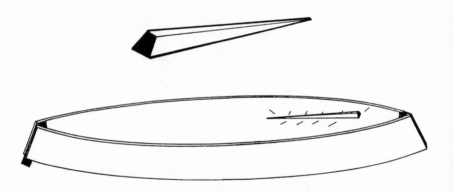

Fitting the Skeg

Fitting the skeg, the next to last step, requires the boat to be turned upside down again. The skeg, a 3' directional fin, is placed at the bateau's stern to help the rocker-bottomed craft track in a straight line and to help stabilize the craft in rough water. The skeg measures 3" high at the back and tapers off toward the bow. It is attached to the bottom of the boat about 2' forward of the stern stem.

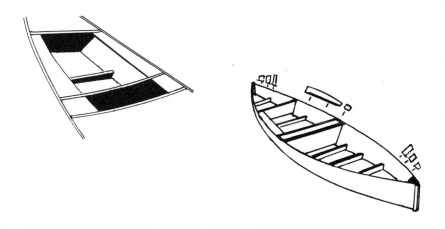

Decking the Bateau

Decking is fitted over the bow and stern and partial decking is placed to frame the live-box and minnow well. A lattice cover for the live-box and a simple seat are made out of strips of cypress and cypress boards. The seat support strips are cut about 14" long to fit snugly between the first bulkhead and the first cross support forward of the first bulkhead.

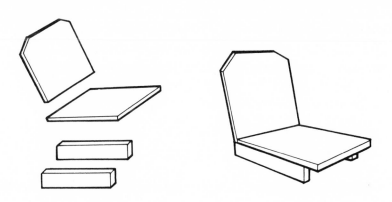

Seat for Bateau

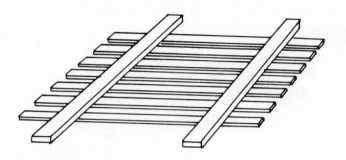

Lattice for Fish Box

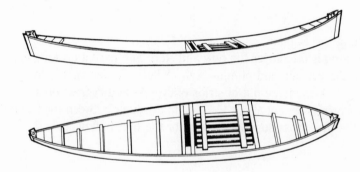

Finished Bateau

Notes

1. William B. Knipmeyer, "Folk Boats of Eastern French Louisiana," in Don Yoder, ed., *American Folklife* (Austin, Texas: University of Texas Press, 1977), 130.
2. *Rocker* is the upward curvature of the keel line from the center toward the ends of the boat.
3. *Flare* is a term used to describe a hull cross-section that grows increasingly wider as it rises from the waterline toward the tops of the sides.
4. Moore and Martin soon established a pattern for working together that they followed throughout the boat construction. Moore would begin a unit of work with his hand tools, and Martin would finish it with his electric power tools. Most of the actual sawing and nailing, etc., was done by Martin under the direct supervision of Moore. To avoid confusion of names, we have prepared this narrative using Moore as the sole active agent in the construction process, except when Martin introduced an innovation to the boat-building, such as the use of silicone caulking to seal the seams.
5. Construction of the boat is done with bottom up until the latter stages. Only after the bottom has been fitted is the boat turned right side up.
6. Galbraith, who taught Moore much about boatbuilding, laid his cross supports down flat in the boat. Moore explains why Galbraith did this, as well as why he chooses not to follow his old mentor on this minor point. "If you noticed [in the old Galbraith-made boat] he had some in the back standing up, but there where the man set he didn't like to have that high thing interfere with his feet all day long. But when you put them cross supports flat in there, they aren't very strong up and down, and the nails go through [the cross supports laid down flat], so you have to clinch them and they come loose."
7. Moore says he likes to use a single 20" red cypress plank for the bottom of this bateau design.
8. Ideally, the bottom boards should be a little thinner than the side boards, because it is difficult, according to Moore, to nail two boards together on the edge if they are the same thickness.

All photographs reproduced by permission of Stan Godwin © 1983.

Contributors

Francis Edward Abernethy is Professor of English at Stephen F. Austin State University and is the Secretary-Editor of the Texas Folklore Society.

Blake Wiley Burleson of Waco is a Ph.D. candidate in religious history at Baylor. He has done considerable travel and research in primitive religion among the tribes in East Africa.

Rosa Amelia del Valle Chazarreta of San Miguel de Tucuman, Argentina, received an M.A. in English at Hardin-Simmons University and is now a Ph.D. candidate in comparative literature at Texas Tech.

Lawrence Clayton of Abilene is Professor of English and Dean of the College of Arts and Sciences at Hardin-Simmons University. He is also a past president and a regular contributor to the Society's volumes and programs.

James H. Conrad of Commerce is archivist and oral historian at East Texas State University.

Joe Graham of Millican is Professor of English at Texas A&M. He was born and raised in the Big Bend of far-west Texas, learned to play guitar, and became president of the Texas Folklore Society.

John Graves of Glen Rose, author of *Goodbye to a River, Hard Scrabble,* "The Last Running," and other treasures, is the Dean of Texas Writers.

James Ward Lee of Denton is a past president of the Society and is Professor of English at North Texas State University.

Al Lowman of Stringtown is a research associate at the Institute of Texan Cultures in San Antonio who has produced a considerable volume of work on the history, folklore, and art of Texas and the Southwest.

Elton Miles of Alpine is a past president of the Society and is Professor Emeritus of English at Sul Ross State University, having served thirty-one years on that faculty.

Marguerite Nixon of Beaumont and the University of Texas School of Journalism is a poet and short story writer whose work has appeared in *House Beautiful, Guideposts, Capper's Weekly,* and many other magazines and periodicals.

Paul Patterson of Crane, a far-west Texan by birth and preference, has ridden and written about that area for three-fourths of a hundred years and does not intend to change ranges or subjects.

Connie Ricci of Abilene is a mother and school teacher, currently completing her graduate work at Hardin-Simmons University.

Thad Sitton of Austin is an oral historian with the Texas Sesquicentennial Commission. His previous publications include *Oral History: A Guide for Teachers* and *The Loblolly Book*.

Ernest B. Speck of Alpine has been a PTFS contributor since 1944, when he published a folk song he found in his Llano home county. He is a past president of the Society and editor of *Mody Boatright, Folklorist*.

William N. Stokes, Jr., of Dallas is a retired lawyer and the Society's Counselor. He is a frequent contributor to the Society's programs and publications, as well as an author of three books.

Don R. Swadley of the University of Texas at Arlington is a long-time Society contributor and an outstanding singer and guitar picker.

Charles R. Townsend of Canyon and West Texas State University is the author of *San Antonio Rose: The Life and Music of Bob Wills* and is presently under contract for *A History of Western Swing: From Bob Wills to the Present*.

Index